Klimt: Beethoven

by Jean-Paul Bouillon

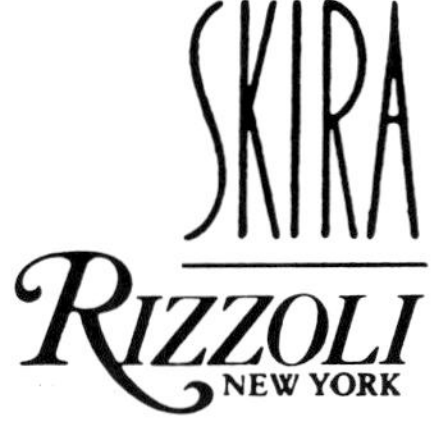

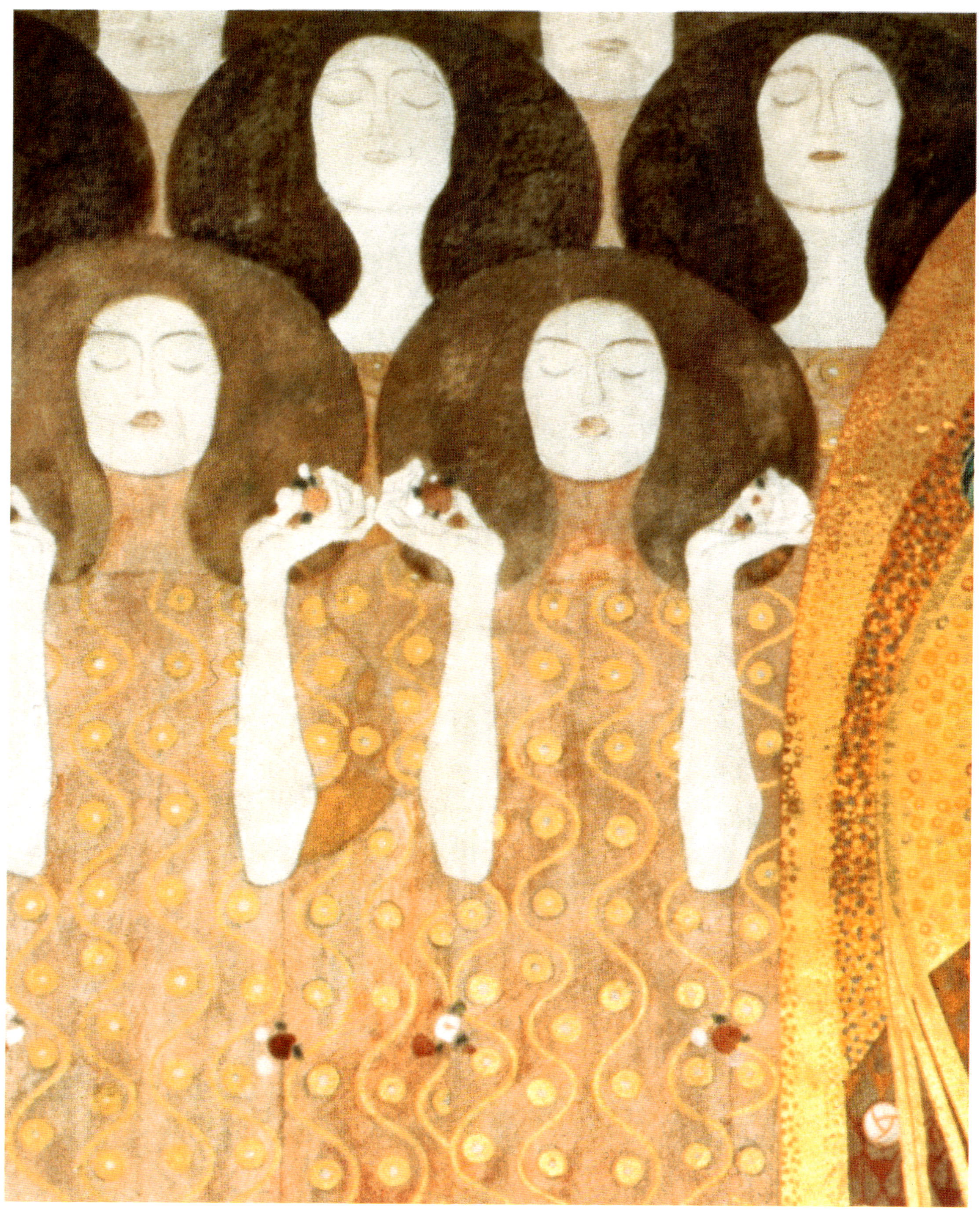

Klimt: Beethoven

BETWEEN 1895 and 1918, the year of his death, the work of Klimt, who was born in Vienna in 1862, had a runaway success which raised it to the heights of international Art Nouveau. Its focal point was the Beethoven Frieze painted in 1902 for the fourteenth exhibition of the Secession group founded by the painter five years earlier. It is a famous and little-known work which has only recently reappeared in all its splendour after lengthy, patient restoration. Published here in full for the first time since its resurrection, it becomes obvious that it is the painter's key work. It combines his central motifs and brings his main themes together for the greater glory of form. As Ludwig Hevesi, the most perceptive contemporary critic, wrote at the time, it is undoubtedly Klimt's masterpiece and it now resumes its rightful place among the major works of art at the turn of the century.

I
Background

THE fourteenth exhibition of the Secession, in which Gustav Klimt's Beethoven Frieze played a major role, opened in Vienna on 15 April 1902 in a strategically placed city at a crucial moment. Since these twin factors largely determined its significance, it is essential to describe the background in some detail if we are to grasp how place and time had their effect.

Established five years previously as a reaction against the smug conservatism of the House of Artists (Künstlerhaus), the Vienna Secession, like its German predecessors, was clearly based on a break with academic tradition, but owing to the exceptional position of the Austro-Hungarian monarchy during the period it did not enjoy the same status or have the same function as the avant-gardes of the rest of Europe. Between her defeat at Sadowa (1866) and the disintegration attendant on the 1914-1918 war, Austria was faced with insoluble problems of her own, primarily those posed by the medley of different nationalities which left her constantly in doubt about her real identity. All hope of a rational solution disappeared with the decline and fall (1879) of the dominant German Liberal party supported by the mass of the secular bourgeoisie. The appearance of new forces (on the left, Victor Adler's Social Democratic workers' party, formed in 1888, and Karl Lueger's Christian Socialist league established a year later with middle-class backing; on the right, a Pan-Germanic party) left the Emperor no option but to pursue a course of compromise and pragmatism.

In an attempt to preserve the fiction of imperial unity in the face of the growing class struggle and increasing nationalist demands, economic growth and the development of cultural policy under the aegis of enlightened despotism became the priorities of Ernst von Körber's cabinet, especially his Minister of Culture, Wilhelm von Hartel, between 1900 and 1904. This was a brief period of calm between the uprisings of 1897 precipitated by a proposal to reform the linguistic statute and the general strike of 1905, which marked the irresistible rise of the Social Democratic party—two events foreshadowing the ultimate disaster.

So beyond its specifically artistic aims, the Secession was involved from the start in wider cultural conflicts in which its problems of form were very much at stake. The younger generation's revolt against its parents (Klimt, the group's first president, was born in Vienna in 1862) actually took place to promote a higher order of things in an attempt to save the health of the nation by the creation of a "typically Austrian" Art Nouveau (the words used by Hermann Bahr when he hailed *Schubert at the Piano* in 1899). Indeed, after Franz Joseph was forced to accept Karl Lueger's triumphal election as Mayor of Vienna the year before, the Emperor personally opened the first Secession exhibition in March 1898. In the following year Josef Hoffmann, and shortly afterwards Kolo Moser and Alfred Roller, two other eminent members of the group, were appointed Professors at the School of Decorative Arts. In the spring of 1900 the seventh exhibition attracted no less than 38,000 visitors and although some of Klimt's pictures, such as his *Pallas Athene* of 1898, had already created a scandal, others, such as the *Schubert* of 1899, were given a triumphant reception.

But this progressive integration was precarious, the understanding with those in power ambiguous and the phase of ascendancy a brief one. The government's effort to cement national unity by cultural means could not stand up to the test of harsher realities. Körber, too, fell in November 1904, his cabinet foundering on the nationality question. The year before, *Ver Sacrum*, the Secession's review, was forced to cease publication for lack of public support. The present belonged to the Christian Socialist petty bourgeoisie of Karl Lueger, the future to the Social Democrats, neither of which had any use for an aestheticizing avant-garde. The Empire was irrevocably doomed to national, political and aesthetic disruption.

The internal history of the Secession faithfully mirrors the fate of this impossible utopia, from the democratic aspirations of its beginnings, from the hopes placed in national reconciliation and the regeneration of society by the power of forms alone, to the inevitable conflicts (especially between Stylists and Naturalists) which led Klimt and his friends to leave the Secession in 1905, the very year in which the general strike gave the death blow to the illusion of social consensus.

But during this brief intense experience, the Secession, the last group to join the movement, concentrated and summed up the whole conceptual world of Art Nouveau just when it was tottering.

It inherited Art Nouveau's mantle between the ambiguities of the Paris World's Fair of 1900, when a fashion was changing, and the 1902 Turin Exhibition of Modern Decorative Art, the venue for one last ephemeral triumph, significantly held in an architectural setting which was Austrian in the extreme. It was then that the works of the great exiles, Hodler and Mackintosh, sought refuge in Vienna.

Lastly, Klimt's own career within the group—even more than that of Otto Wagner—summed up in turn that moment of hope which ended in bitter disappointment, and the 1902 frieze came at its most melodramatic moment, namely when the long drawn out affair of the three ceiling panels for the University commissioned from the painter in 1896 had reached a crisis before the final refusal of them.

The first two panels, *Philosophy* (awarded a gold medal in Paris in 1900, but fiercely attacked in the same year at the Secession's seventh exhibition), and *Medicine* (centre of a scandal comparable to the tenth exhibition in 1901), had just proved by their nonconformist iconography, and even more so by a spatial organization which was the absolute negation of the hierarchy of values they were supposed to illustrate, that the fundamental conservatism of the body social could not accommodate a formal proposition so radically opposed to its basic ideological concepts. After the savage polemics which ensued, Hartel, the Minister of Culture, gave Klimt only lukewarm support and in the same year (1901) he refused to confirm the painter's election to the Academy of Fine Arts.

When Klimt resumed work on his third panel, *Jurisprudence*, he transformed the triumphant allegory of the preliminary sketch into a vigorous indictment of his critics, notably by reversing the proportion of the areas reserved for the forces of Good and Evil. This was a deliberately provocative gesture, as was the contemporaneous *Goldfish* shown at the thirteenth exhibition in February 1902, which was intended as a deliberate slap in the face for public taste. Rejection of the whole ceiling commission was inevitable and Klimt finally withdrew his works in 1905, the year when he himself left the Secession, when Körber had fallen and when increasing dangers finally put paid to the hope of salvation by art.

All that remained for Klimt, with the support of a few patrons, was an egocentric retreat to the values whose synthesis he had effected in tandem: the values of life as a celebration of universal Eros and of art considered as a purely formal organization of "plastic equivalents," to use the phrase coined by Maurice Denis in 1890. 1902 was also the year when the portrait of Emilie Flöge, Klimt's mistress and "beneficent goddess," marked a turning point, with the sexualized ornamentation which took possession of the body of the loved one and incorporated it into the strict homogeneous organization of the canvas, but without removing any of the sensuality of its real existence. The sexualization of life (contrary to the official morality of a society in which Klimt was now in a marginal position) has rejoined the formalization of the picture. From now on it is an intrinsic part of it.

Even before we attempt to dismantle its complicated mechanisms, we must realize that the Beethoven Frieze comes at the centre of an astonishing series of interconnected circumstances, all requiring different levels of interpretation. They include the saga of Art Nouveau, then at its turning point, between the 1900 fair in Paris and the 1902 exhibition in Turin; the concentration of its aesthetic aims in Vienna as exemplified in the history of the Secession between its foundation in 1897 and Klimt's departure in 1905; its special significance under the Körber government between 1900 and 1904 for the destiny of the Austro-Hungarian Empire divided between "dream and reality"; the middle period of Klimt's life during the dramatic passage from *Medicine* to *Jurisprudence*; and lastly the point where Eros and Art find one of their most fascinating conjunctions.

The manifold meanings of the Beethoven Frieze are to be sought in this union, and the fact that it was originally meant to be an ephemeral decoration destined for destruction—whereas *it* is reborn today and the University panels have disappeared for ever in the chaos of the Second World War—is just one more paradox. For Klimt, for Vienna, for the whole of Art Nouveau, it was clearly a unique, ephemeral and uncertain, fragile and precious moment.

II
Context

It is true that the fourteenth Secession exhibition was always intended to be ephemeral, but it was the general conception that changed later. As Ernst Stöhr wrote in the foreword to the catalogue, the idea was to substitute for the original principle of organization, which consisted in the "harmonious grouping of heterogeneous parts," a unified ensemble in which paintings and sculptures would be "at the service of the idea of space" (*Raumidee*), to "submit the parts to the idea of the whole" by obeying the "inexorable logic imposed by intensification of the spatial character (*Raumcharakter*) and holding firm to a single guiding idea." This desire for unification carries on the search for synthesis undertaken by the pioneers of Art Nouveau. It was what Mackintosh in Glasgow and Van de Velde in Germany had both been working towards since 1899 (works by both of them were shown at the eighth exhibition in the autumn of 1900). In the ninth exhibition the plaster of Rodin's *Burghers of Calais* had already been shown in a much lighter and highly theatrical way in a setting by Alfred Roller. At the tenth, in 1901, Kolo Moser provided a unique and ordered architectural framework for showing the pictures. In 1902, the synthesis culminated in the "highest and best of what men of all ages have been able to offer: temple art" (*Tempelkunst*), which fulfils "what our time proposes to the creative aspiration of the artist: the conscious organization of an inner space" (*die zielbewusste Ausgestaltung eines Innenraumes*). The fact that this work was provisional, condemned in advance by the exhibitions which would succeed it, mattered little. "We want to learn," to "experience the grace (*Segen*) of a work which has a design and a goal," was the artists' message.

Logic, necessity, submission to a unifying program: we hear a distant echo of the principles of Viollet-le-Duc at the beginnings of Art Nouveau. But in Vienna after 1900, it functioned in the state of pure art, so to speak, for the glorification and "grace" of its execution in practice.

Still to be found was the governing idea of a temple which could no longer be the temple of the Church (especially the Church of Karl Lueger's Christian Socialists), but the temple of art, and art alone. That explains the choice of Max Klinger's *Beethoven*, a large-scale sculpture begun in embryo in 1886 and not finished until

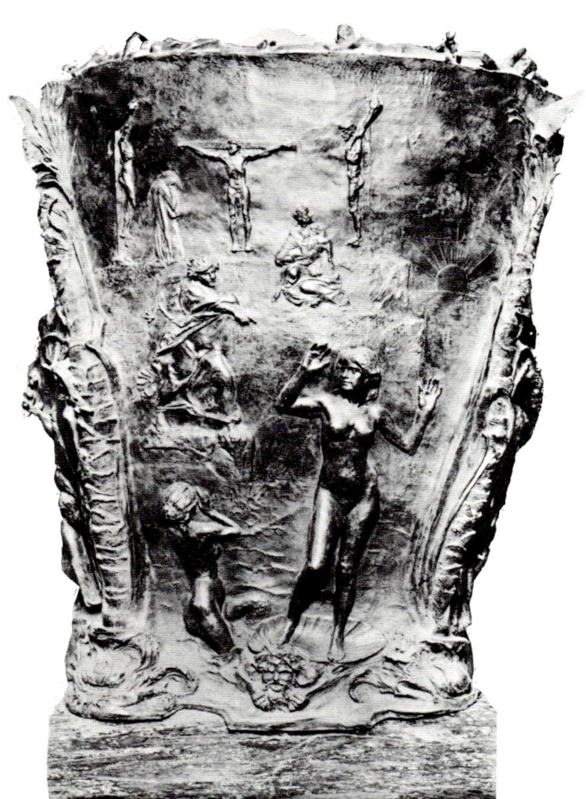

Max Klinger (1857-1920): Back of the Beethoven Throne, 1902, with Crucifixion and Birth of Venus. Bronze.

March 1902. Internal space could only be deployed around a work of art which was at once its anticipation, projection and reflection. Homage (from the Secession artists) to a homage (from Klinger to Beethoven), the 1902 exhibition raised to its apogee the "will to art" which underlies the progress of European avant-gardes from the late 1880s and finds its ultimate expression in Vienna.

Why the choice of Klinger, whose heavy symbolism, insistent iconography and massive execution might seem worlds away from the delicate work of the Viennese, or Rodin, to whom Klimt was close in many respects? The German sculptor, a correspondent of the Secession, influenced its members in two ways, by his own example and by his theories as set out in an important work published in 1891 (*Malerei und Zeichnung*), partly taken up again in the 1902 catalogue and in which the two main principles of Art Nouveau are reaffirmed: the higher value of an art which takes into consideration the totality of space (*Raumkunst*) and the need for the specific treatment of different materials in order to achieve style. Klinger's *Beethoven* provides an example of this, with its carefully chosen precious stones and marbles, which, whatever we may think of them today, had the primary function of dissolving a sense of reality so that a style could flourish. At the same time, it re-echoes the classical example: it is a case of responding to the *Zeus* of Phidias and so rediscovering its sacred character *by form*.

The very *image* of the *Beethoven* in its heroic nudity, with clenched fist and gazing into the beyond in creative thought, sums up the meaning of the whole work. He is the hero, martyr and redeemer of mankind, following the interpretation formulated by Wagner and Nietzsche, which we find again in Bourdelle's great tragic mask of *Beethoven* (Metropolitan Museum, New York), also dating to 1902, and in the celebrated brief *Life of Beethoven* written by Romain Rolland in the same year.

Klinger's iconography even goes a little further, with symbolic imagery on the three surfaces of the bronze throne where classical and Christian worlds confront each other. This stands out on the back of the throne where the Crucifixion is opposed, by St. John's dramatic gesture, to the birth of Venus, herself a promise of pagan redemption by Beauty. On the throne the Artist has become the

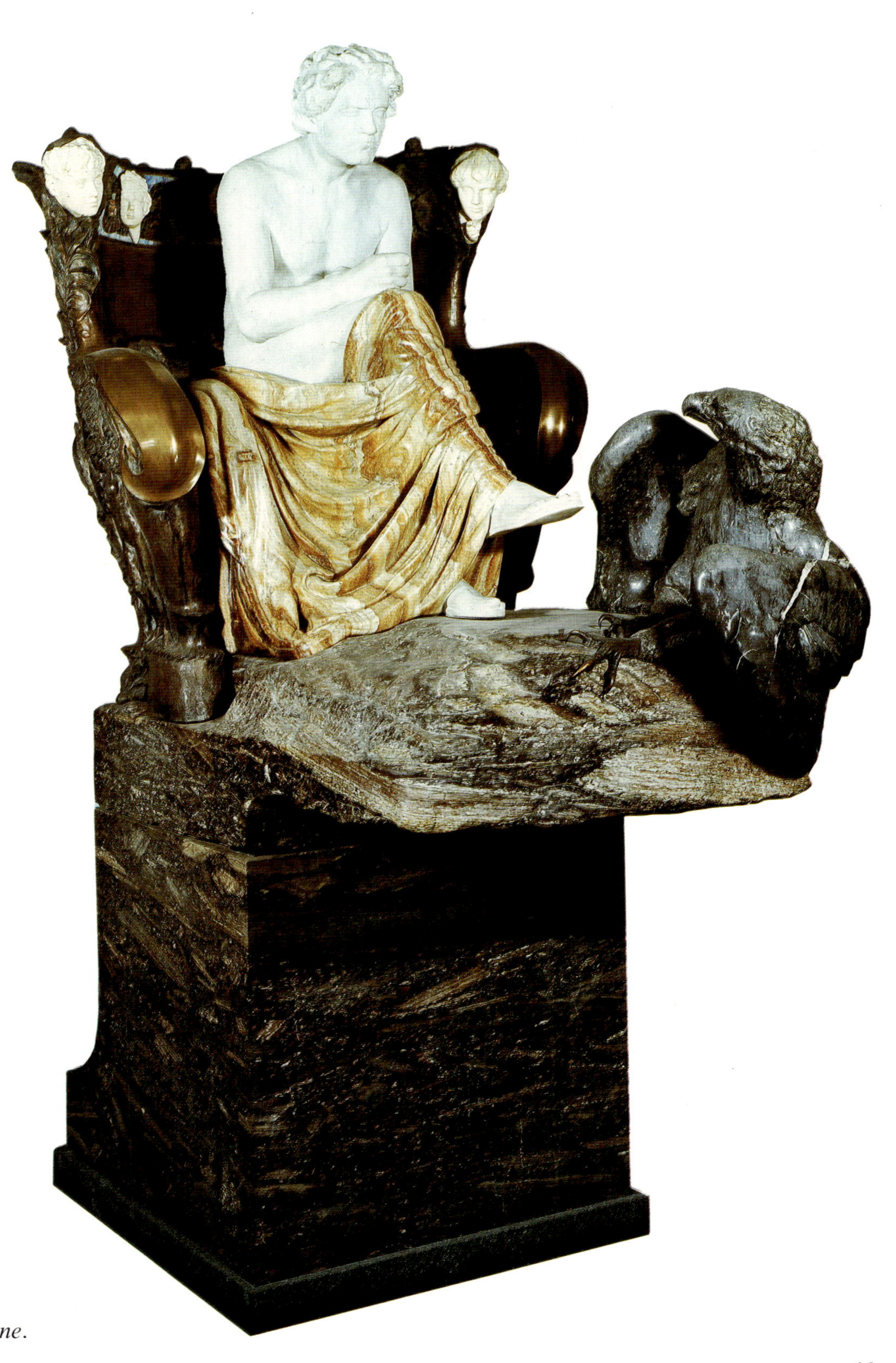

Max Klinger (1857-1920):
Statue of Beethoven, 1902.
Marble of various kinds, with bronze throne.

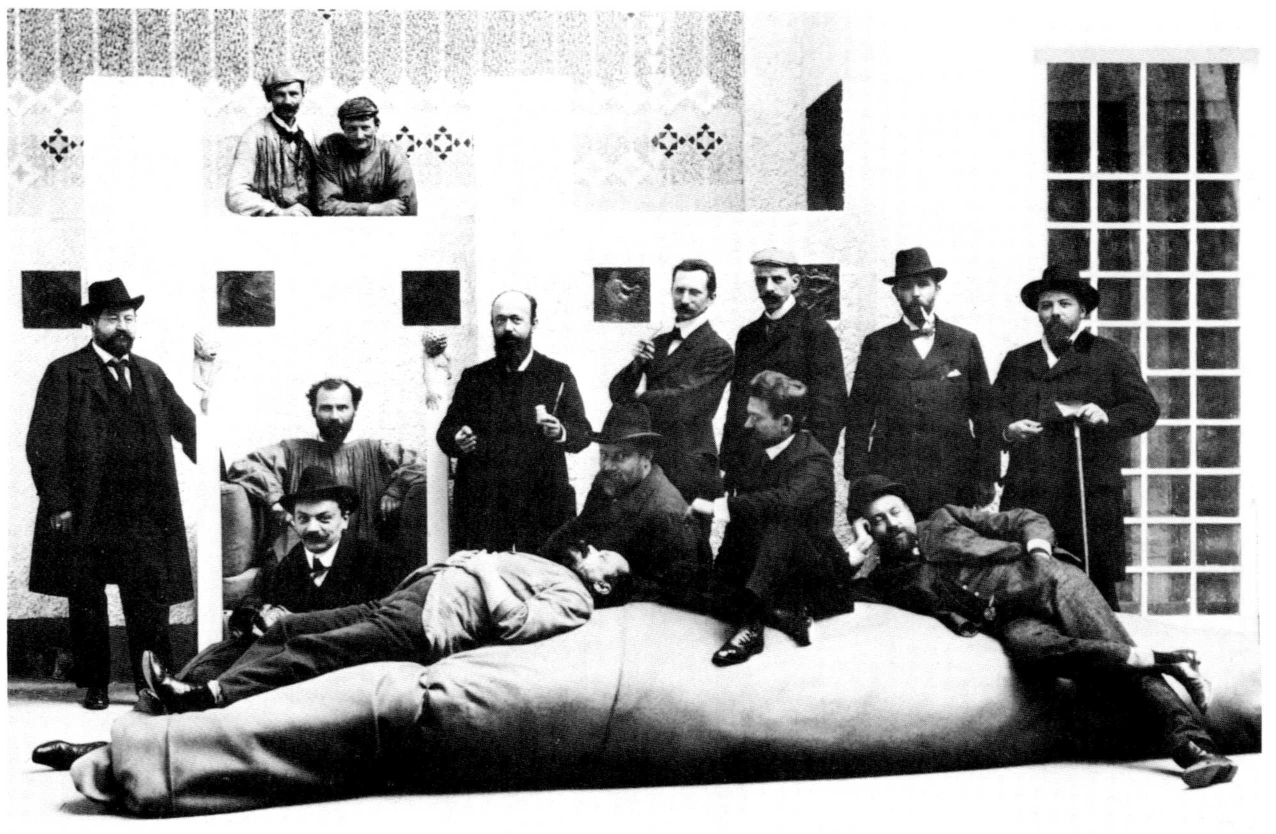

Members of the Vienna Secession at the Beethoven Exhibition, 1902.
Left to right: Anton Stark, Gustav Klimt (seated),
Kolo Moser (in front of Klimt, with hat), Adolf Böhm,
Maximilian Lenz (lying on his back), Ernst Stöhr
(with hat), Wilhelm List, Emil Orlik (seated), Maximilian
Kurzweil (with cap), Leopold Stolba, Carl Moll (lying down), Rudolf Bacher.

veritable Messiah of the contemporary world and surpasses that sterile confrontation of which Klinger had made a first version in his great *Christ on Olympus* of 1897, exhibited at the 1899 Secession. As Franz Servaes wrote in his 1902 monograph on the sculptor (with the *Beethoven* as a frontispiece and the first reproduction of the bust of Nietzsche), the work clearly announces a "Third Reich," that of Art beyond the conflict between Dionysus and Christ Crucified.

So form and content meet, or attempt to meet, in the *Beethoven*, whose outward appearance proclaims the original symbolic concept with which it is imbued. Thus in the words of Ernst Stöhr it "anticipates the fulfilment" of the master idea desired by the members of the Secession. Now all they had to do was to build a suitable temple around this "flamboyant jewel" and provide it with a systematic and "highly conscious" program, which, in spite of the obvious difference in artistic ability of the twenty-one participants, would turn the ensemble into an organic whole from which Klimt's frieze could not and should not be separated.

Here the internal architecture conceived by Hoffmann, who was in charge of the overall artistic direction, played an essential part by putting the final touch to the Secession Building built by Joseph Olbrich in 1898 (already a "temple" because of its simple volumes and pronounced austerity as opposed to the "profane" historicist ornateness of the buildings in the Ring). Olbrich had deliberately left the interior empty and open, giving no artistic expression to the motto chosen by the artists to appear on the pediment: "To every age its Art, to Art its freedom" (*Der Zeit ihre Kunst, Der Kunst ihre Freiheit*). So the art of the period was still to

Joseph Maria Olbrich (1867-1908):
The Secession Building, Vienna, 1898. Photograph of c. 1940.

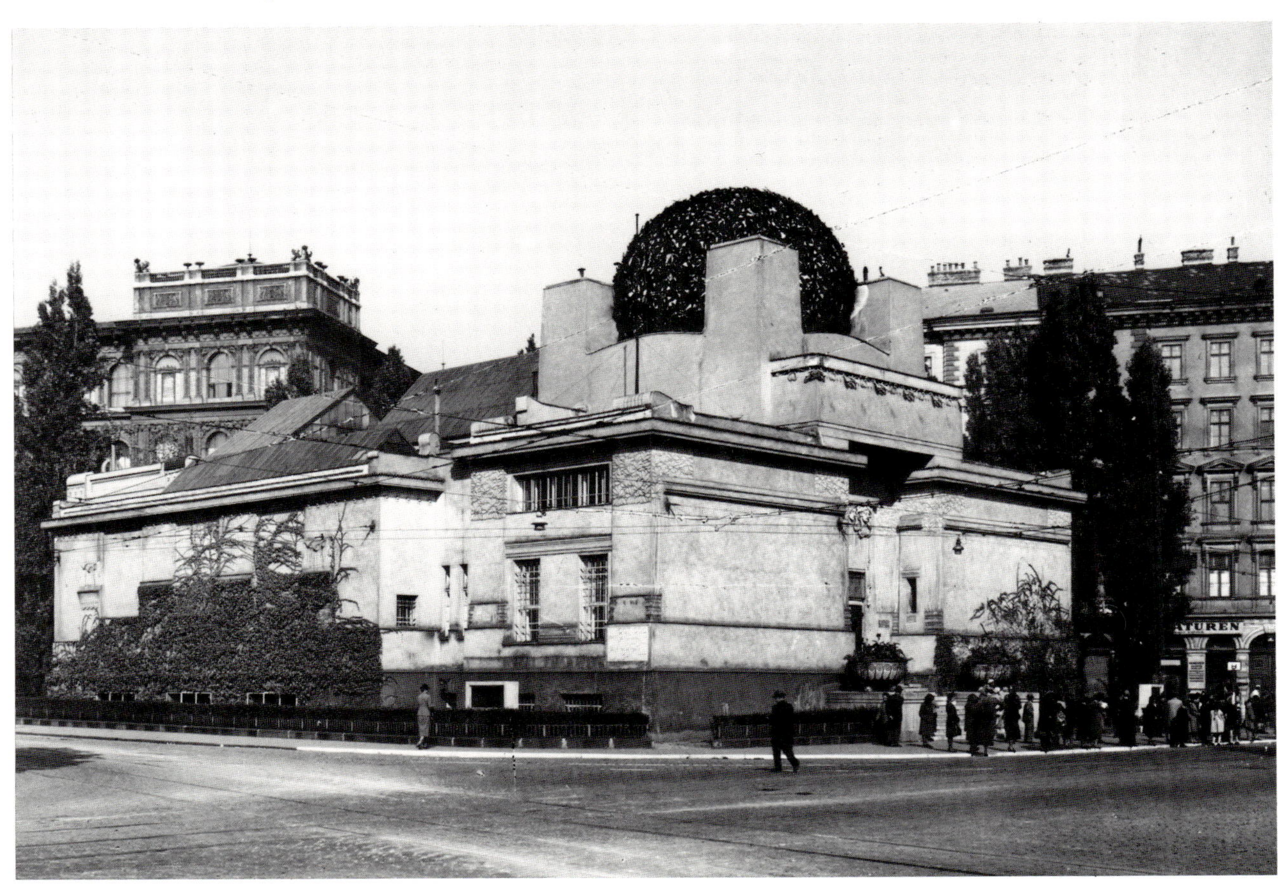

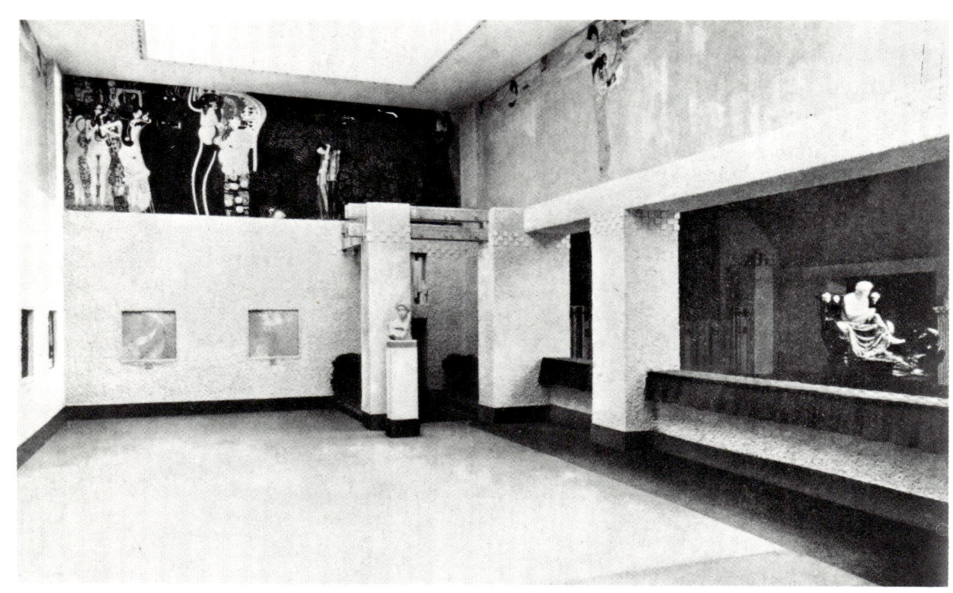

Klimt Room at the Beethoven Exhibition, 1902, with partial view of Klimt's frieze. Right, Max Klinger's Beethoven.

be found and the revolutionary system of movable internal partitions finally chosen was in itself an invitation to examine the various propositions of international art. In 1902 the Secession had adequately fulfilled its function as "welcoming space"; now it had to make its own proposition by sealing the union of its community in the completion of the "temple" dreamt of ten years earlier by the French Nabis, those western "prophets" of the Art Nouveau which had now sought refuge in Vienna.

Hoffmann's brief contribution to the catalogue points out everything that the interior installation owes to his principles: the use of "authentic materials," "energetic rejection of make-believe and lies, the greatest possible simplicity in the language of materials and forms." The neo-primitive character of the "shrine" and its obvious reference to archaic art (Mycenaean palace, Etruscan tomb, Christian basilica) thus result less from the intention to copy a model than from an aesthetic and at the same time moral bias which is quite typical of Art Nouveau. This applies equally to the execution, primarily based on the notion of contrast: raw plaster, which was inexpensive and also served to bring the walls alive, opposed to smooth surfaces, to show off the articulations; the deliberate and emphasized plainness of this basic material, white (with a grey ground), to accentuate the precious works mounted in it; a golden light diffused by awnings in the side halls as opposed to the bright overhead lighting of the central hall. The "hallowing" (as in theory with the Klinger) was supposed to come from the treatment of form and not from a pre-existing symbolic concept. The division of this space, especially its structural organization, by a route which

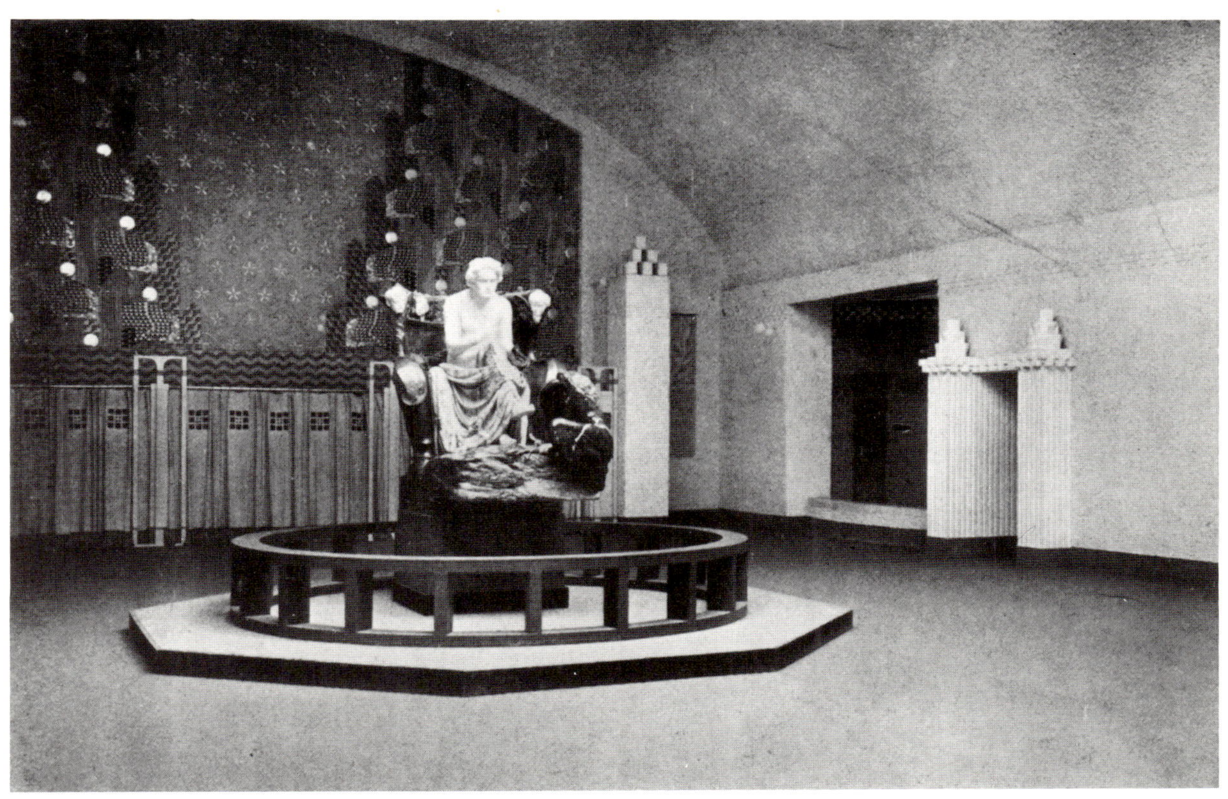

Main room of the Beethoven Exhibition with Max Klinger's Beethoven *and Alfred Roller's mural painting* Sinking Night.

Main room of the Beethoven Exhibition with Max Klinger's Beethoven *(from behind) and Adolf Böhm's mural painting* Dawning Day. *Right, the Klimt Room.*

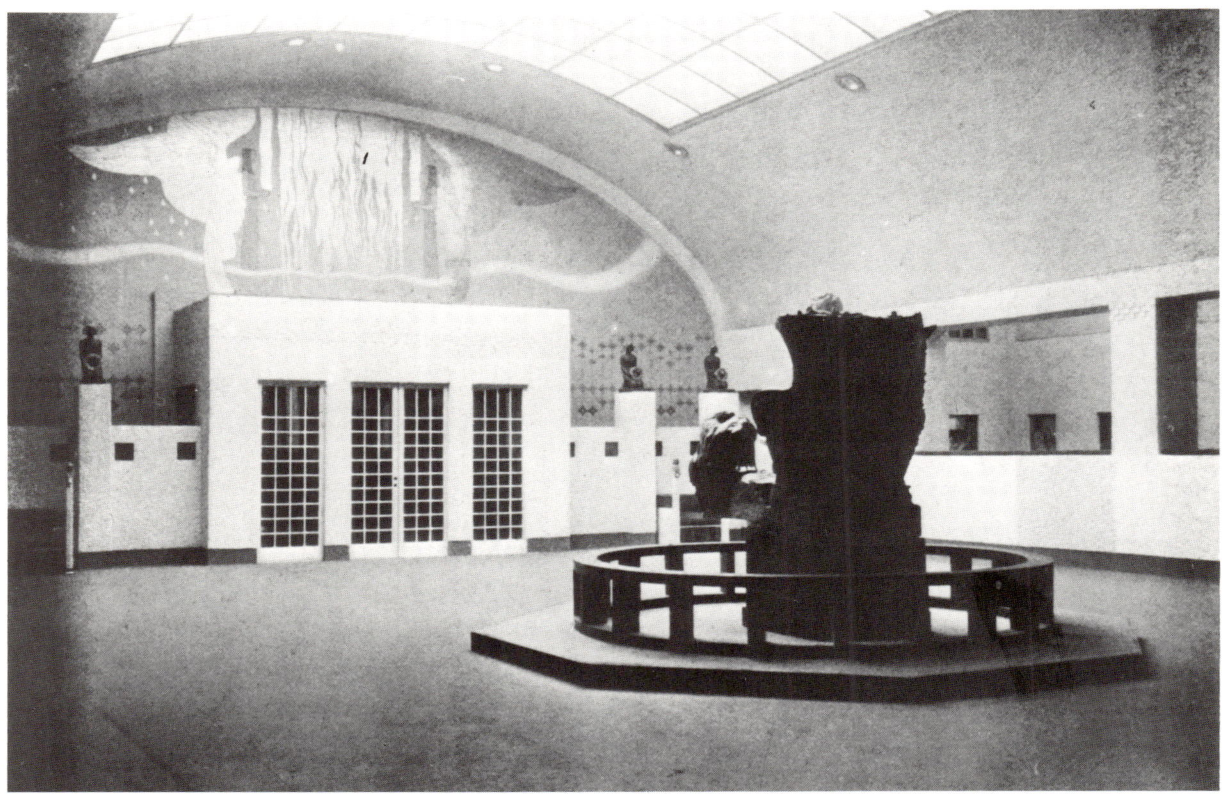

the visitor had to follow (briefly indicated in the catalogue by a diagram marked with arrows) left him no choice but to integrate himself with the layout and bring it to life by his own movement, thus completing the temple by the ritual being celebrated in it. Three "naves" opened out beyond the vestibule and the two side ones were

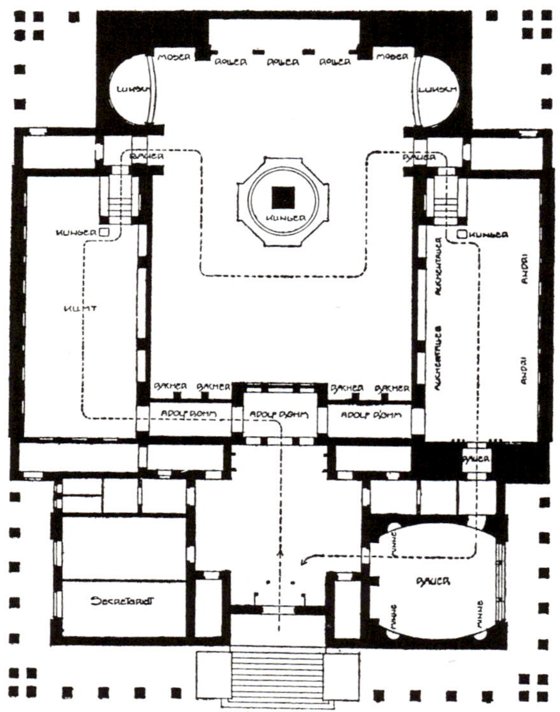

◁ *Plan of the Beethoven Exhibition, from the catalogue of 1902.*

▷ *Alfred Roller (1864-1935): Poster for the Beethoven Exhibition, 1902. Colour lithograph.*

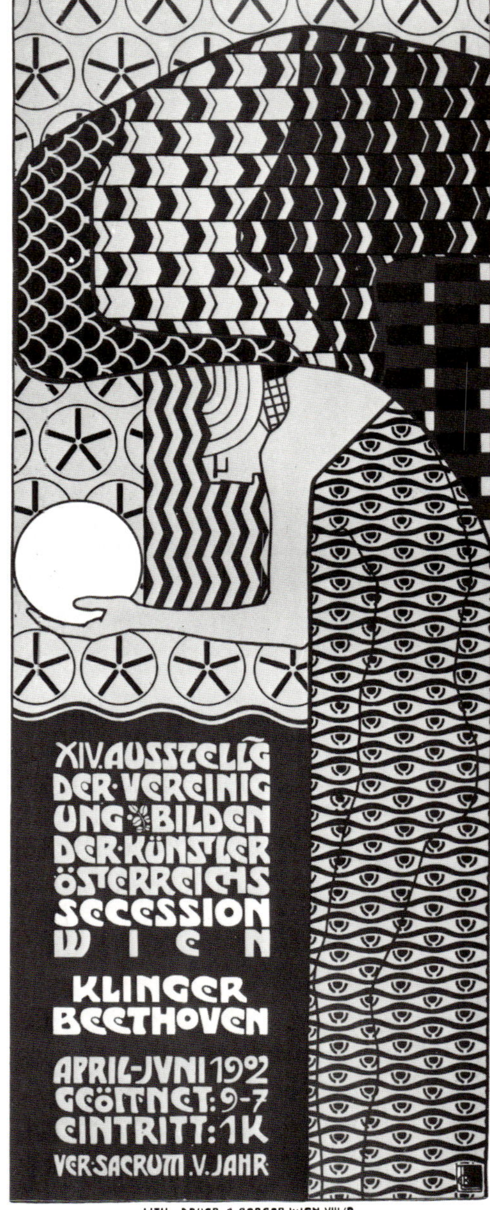

"naves" opened out beyond the vestibule and the two side ones were slightly elevated (at great expense). Most of the works of art were exhibited in them, leaving the Klinger in almost solitary splendour in the middle of the central hall in the "peace desired." But the side rooms also opened on to it at three points, "reinforcing its significance." "The visitor is not led into the presence of the work without preparation: it will have first been seen from a distance and an elevated viewpoint," the catalogue remarks, and the *Neue Freie Presse* sums up the effect produced: "Prepared by every possible means for an act of devotion (*Andacht*), you reached the statue in a sort of hypnotic state."

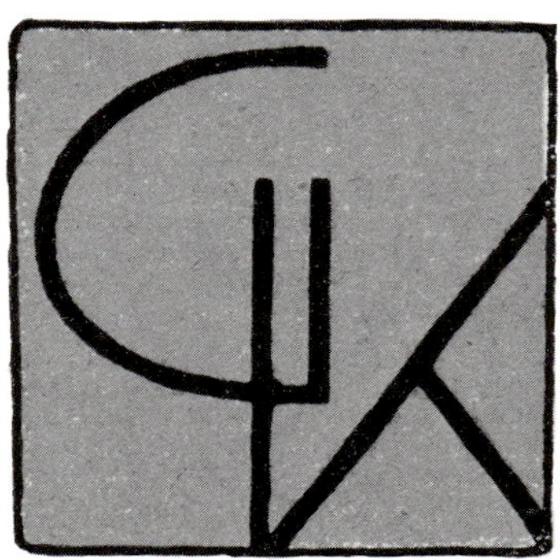

Starting from this strategic occupation of the interior space there developed a complicated network of correspondences between the different works around the Klinger intended to scale down its effect. Thus, in the central hall, we find the large painted panels, *Dawning Day* by Adolf Böhm, which faces the statue, and *Sinking Night* by Alfred Roller placed behind it, with an obvious symbolic significance. And the repeated figures of Roller's panel, those young girls with dangling hair bearing a white disc, find an echo in the beautiful exhibition poster which emphasizes its resolve to remain firmly two-dimensional, its desire to respect the wall and at the same time not to encroach on the volume which belongs by right to the Klinger and the spiritual space it animates around it. In the other axis, Klimt's hall, to the left, replies to the decorations of those of the right with the same Beethovenesque themes, *Joy, Beautiful Divine Spark* by Josef Maria Auchentaller and *Man's Courage and Delight in the Struggle* by Ferdinand Andri. Lastly the medallions vertically embedded in the wall and identified only by the geometric monograms which accompany their brief (purely technical) description in the catalogue echo the friezes above them.

Thus the interior space is unified, arranged and made hierarchical in its three dimensions, with a systematization which seems to outdo even the installations of Mackintosh and Van de Velde. That is undoubtedly one of the meanings of the enigmatic geometric abstract reliefs (the *pure* expression of the concept of space) placed by Hoffmann above the apertures giving access to the central hall from the side rooms. It now remained to animate the whole layout by adding to it the dimension of sound which this "total work of art" still lacked. This was done on 15 April 1902

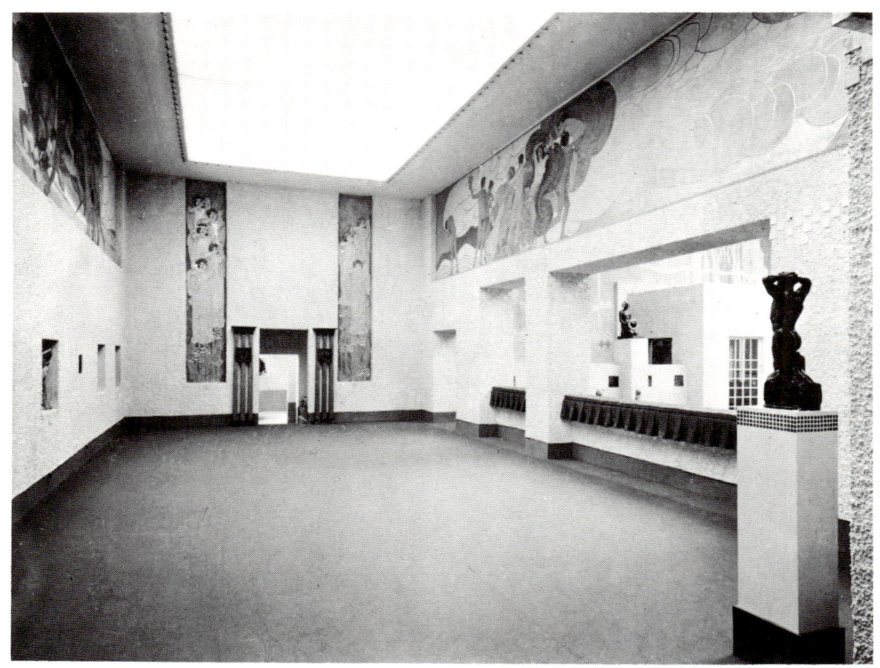

Room on the right at the Beethoven Exhibition. Right wall, the frieze Joy, Beautiful Divine Spark *by J. M. Auchentaller. Far right, Max Klinger's* Athlete.

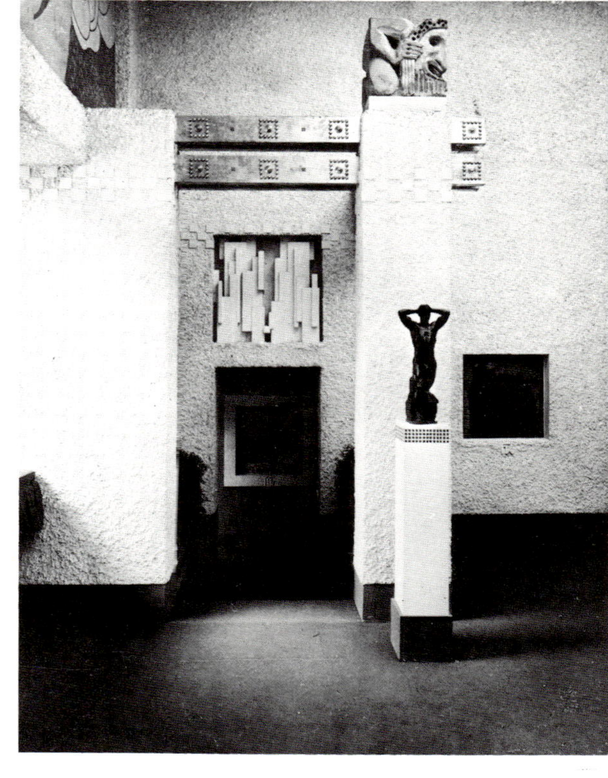

Room on the right at the Beethoven Exhibition with Max Klinger's Athlete *and Josef Hoffmann's abstract relief over the door.*

when Gustav Mahler directed an arrangement for wind instruments and brass of a passage from the finale of the Ninth Symphony in the exhibition building.

Ihr stürzt nieder, Millionen?
Ahnest Du den Schöpfer, Welt?
(Do you prostrate yourselves, you millions?
Do you sense your Creator, world?)

Klinger, who was present, could not restrain his tears, according to Alma Mahler. The mutual celebration of homage to homage, of artists to art and of art to artists was complete. The space had found its moment of truth. "The Act" was at last accomplished. Now this ephemeral fragile assemblage, on which "fleeting existence must not leave its mark" as Stohr wrote in the catalogue, could be dismantled and destroyed. Klinger's work, made of solid lasting raw materials, was naturally excluded from this sacrifice, but Klimt's frieze, apparently the only work to survive today, had a narrow escape.

III
Program

Because it is placed in the left-hand hall at the entrance to the first stage of the visit, the Beethoven Frieze occupies a strategic position. It is the key work. Although it is immediately distinguished from the others by its strength, coherence and the complexity of its internal structure, it is not really at odds with the rest of the program. If anything, it incorporates the program's major original concepts so that it too can dialogue with the Klinger through the three apertures carefully cut out by Hoffmann to allow a view of the statue as soon as the spectator entered the room. But whereas Auchentaller, in the corresponding panel in the right-hand hall, pursues his asymmetrical composition to its conclusion with volutes of clouds, Klimt boldly interrupts his frieze above the four metres of the principal aperture. Let the spectator look and let the Klinger speak for itself, he tells us. And one cannot help recalling the painter's obstinate silence (according to witnesses) when seated next to the sculptor at the banquet on the evening of 15 April 1902. In its diagonal position in relation to the sculpture, the frieze partially takes up its theme again and some of its formal principles (the contrasted use of materials, for example), but ultimately is devoted to the organization of its own system, which does not have exactly the same message with reference to Beethoven.

With Hoffmann, on the other hand, the understanding was deep and total, as it was to be a little later, as an extension of this original experiment, with the mosaics in the dining room of the Palais Stoclet at Brussels. Undoubtedly the position of the frieze adjoining the ceiling on the upper part of the wall is not peculiar to Klimt, since it recurs in the right-hand hall. And it is clear that on this point painter and architect were much impressed by the position (and the comparable decorative section) of the great panel in the Mackintosh room at the eighth Secession exhibition in 1900. But even more than the works of Auchentaller and Andri, not to mention Roller and Böhm, which adhere closely to the *wall*, but do not take into account the actual *character* of the *architecture*, Klimt's frieze instantly impresses by the way it seeks to fit in with the archaic aspect of the decoration, its sacred neo-primitivism, not to say barbarism, which are matched by the hieratic quality and stylization of the frieze's figures, as well as the harsh contrast between

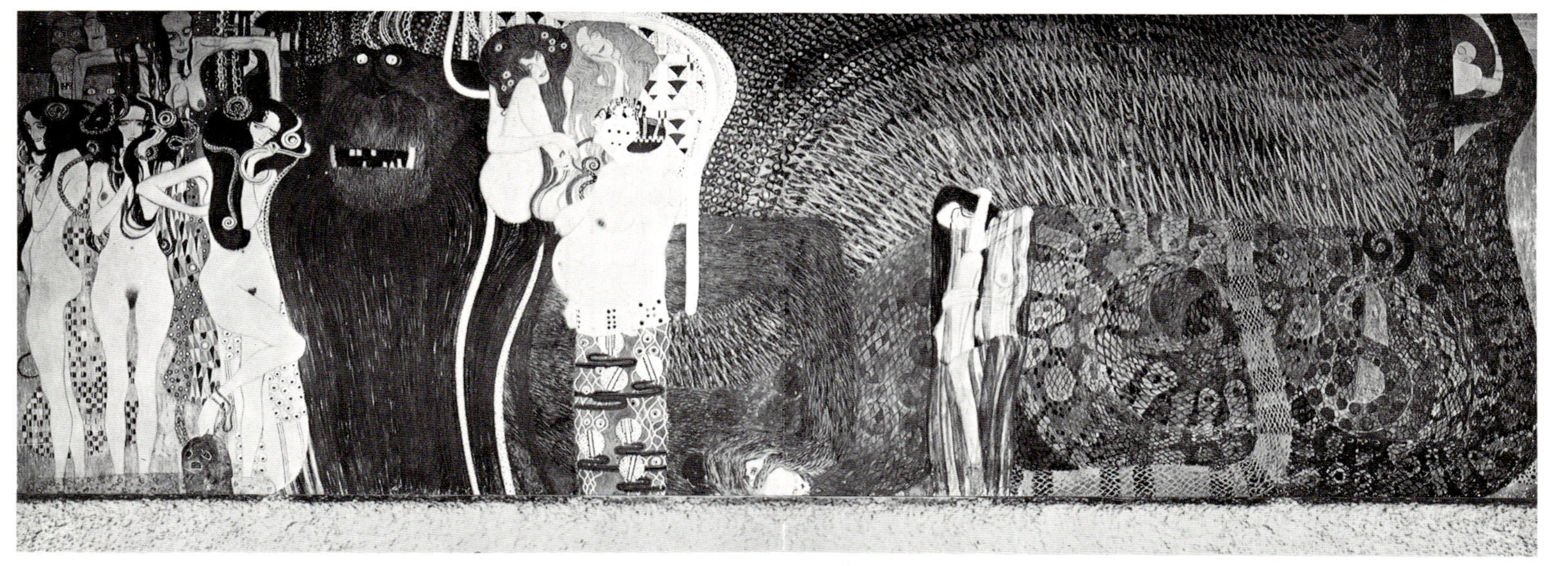

Klimt Room: Overall view of the central wall. Photograph of 1902.

its overall polish, the exoticism of its materials and colours, and the rough plaster surrounding it. This is clearly shown in these fine photographs of 1902 where care has been taken to frame the frieze with some twenty centimetres of the wall which borders it. Klimt's note in the catalogue is brief but explicit on this point: "Decorative principle: regard for the disposition of the room (*Rücksichtnahme auf die Saalanlage*); ornamented plaster surfaces."

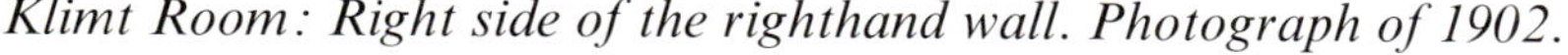

Klimt Room: Right side of the righthand wall. Photograph of 1902.

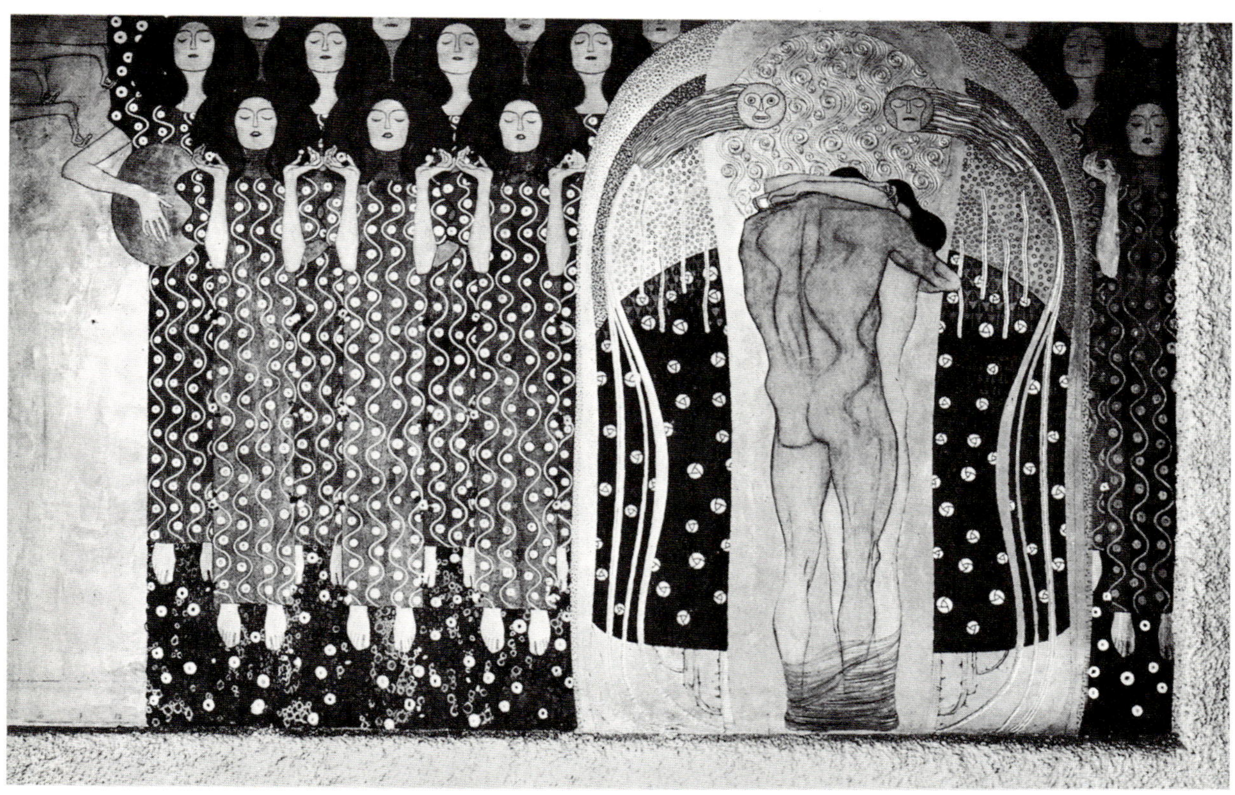

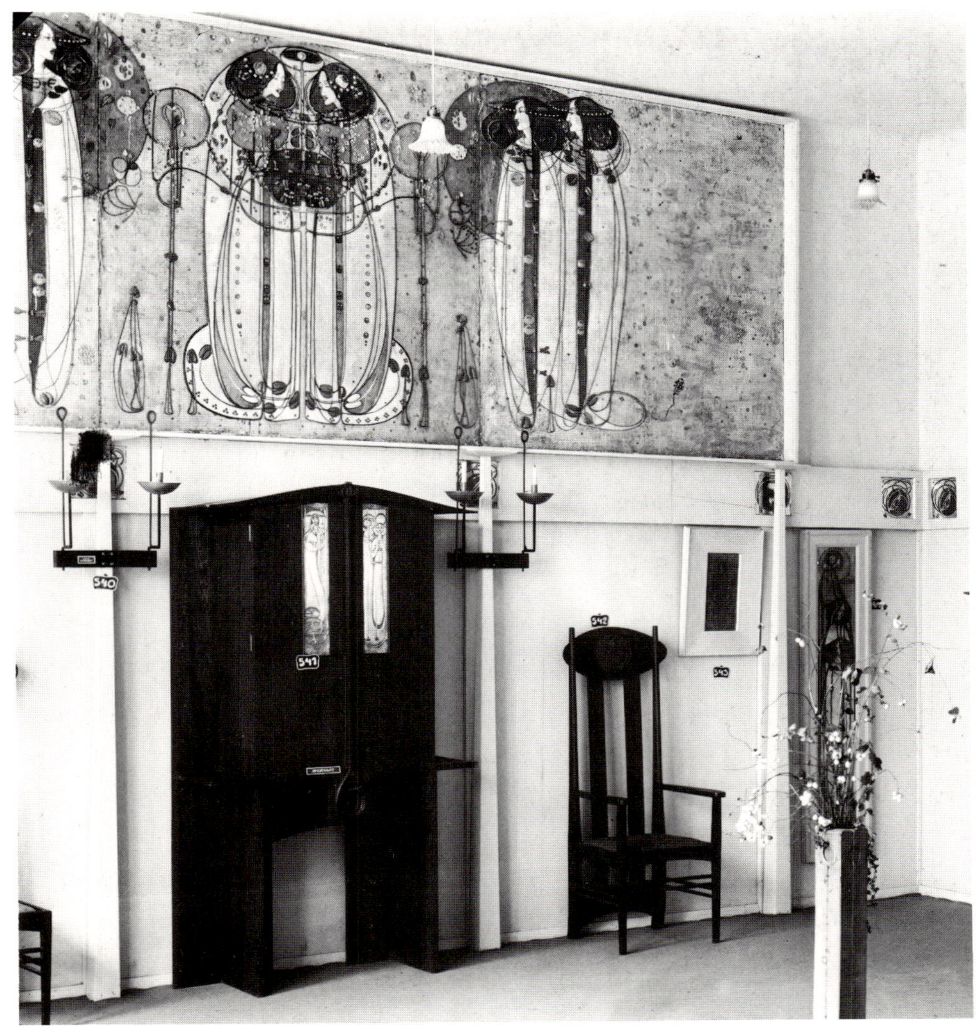

Mackintosh Room at the eighth exhibition of the Vienna Secession, 1900.

One of the functions of the technique and materials used was to contribute to this decorative principle. On a framework of wooden tubing covered with stucco, Klimt did not use fresco painting (as too many commentators originally said in error), but casein colours (in other words tempera on a dry ground, even if it was slightly moistened at the moment of painting); "inlaid stucco and gilding" is all Klimt says, but he also added various inlays and made extensive use of charcoal, graphite and pastel which sometimes give the ensemble the air of a monumental design. By tackling this combination of unusual materials, in an experiment typical of Art Nouveau, Klimt, like Klinger, finds his way towards a style, but he also achieves a privileged agreement with "temple art" as conceived of by Hoffmann.

It is only then that one is allowed access to the actual program of the frieze, mainly covered by the two pages in the catalogue signed at the head with Klimt's monogram. This text is too short and sometimes too vague or ambiguous, but it still provides our main source of information.

Like the exhibition as a whole, of which it is meant to be a microcosm, the frieze first appears as "a coherent sequence" (*eine zusammenhängende Folge*), a sequence which takes the spectator in hand as soon as he enters the room. The point of departure is situated on the wall facing him where the floating figures lead him irresistibly to the right along the first panel. This is "Longing for Happiness" (*Die Sehnsucht nach Glück*), a title which may refer to the wall as a whole or simply to the reclining figures, repeated as a leitmotiv up to the third panel (but not, it seems clear, to the following group alone, as one might have thought until recently on the evidence of the caption of a photograph taken at the 1903 exhibition). About two-thirds of the way along the wall appears a group of six figures, "The Sufferings of Weak Humanity" (*Die Leiden der schwachen Menschheit*), who "beseech the Knight in Armour as external, Pity and Ambition as internal, driving powers, who move the former to undertake the struggle for happiness." The next panel is devoted to "The Hostile Powers" (*Die feindlichen Gewalten*), with

Pages 25 and 26 of the catalogue of the Beethoven Exhibition, explaining the wall paintings.

Linker Seitensaal.

LINKER SEITENSAAL.

WANDMALEREIEN.

DIE MALEREIEN, DIE SICH FRIESARTIG ÜBER DIE OBEREN HÄLFTEN DREIER WÄNDE DIESES SAALES ERSTRECKEN, SIND VON GUSTAV KLIMT OM. MATERIAL: KASEÏNFARBE, AUFgetragener Stuck, Vergoldung. Dekoratives Prinzip: Rücksichtnahme auf die Saalanlage; ornamentierte Putzflächen. Die drei bemalten Wände bilden eine zusammenhängende Folge. Erste Langwand, dem Eingang gegenüber: Die Sehnsucht nach Glück. Die Leiden der schwachen Menschheit: Die Bitten dieser an den wohlgerüsteten Starken als äußere, Mitleid und Ehrgeiz als innere treibende Kräfte, die ihn das Ringen nach dem Glück aufzunehmen bewegen. Schmalwand: Die feindlichen Gewalten. Der

25

Linker Seitensaal.

Gigant Typhoeus, gegen den selbst Götter vergebens kämpften; seine Töchter, die drei Gorgonen. Krankheit, Wahnsinn, Tod. Wollust und Unkeuschheit, Unmäßigkeit. Nagender Kummer. Die Sehnsüchte und Wünsche der Menschen fliegen darüber hinweg. Zweite Langwand: Die Sehnsucht nach Glück findet Stillung in der Poesie. Die Künste führen uns in das ideale Reich hinüber, in dem allein wir reine Freude, reines Glück, reine Liebe finden können. Chor der Paradiesesengel. „Freude, schöner Götterfunke". „Diesen Kuß der ganzen Welt!"

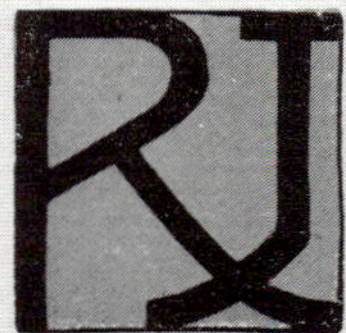

Im linken Seitensaal sind folgende Schmuckplatten in die Wand eingesetzt: Zunächst dem Eingange: RUDOLF JETTMAR OM. Freskomalerei mit Temperaübermalung. Mörtelgrund.

26

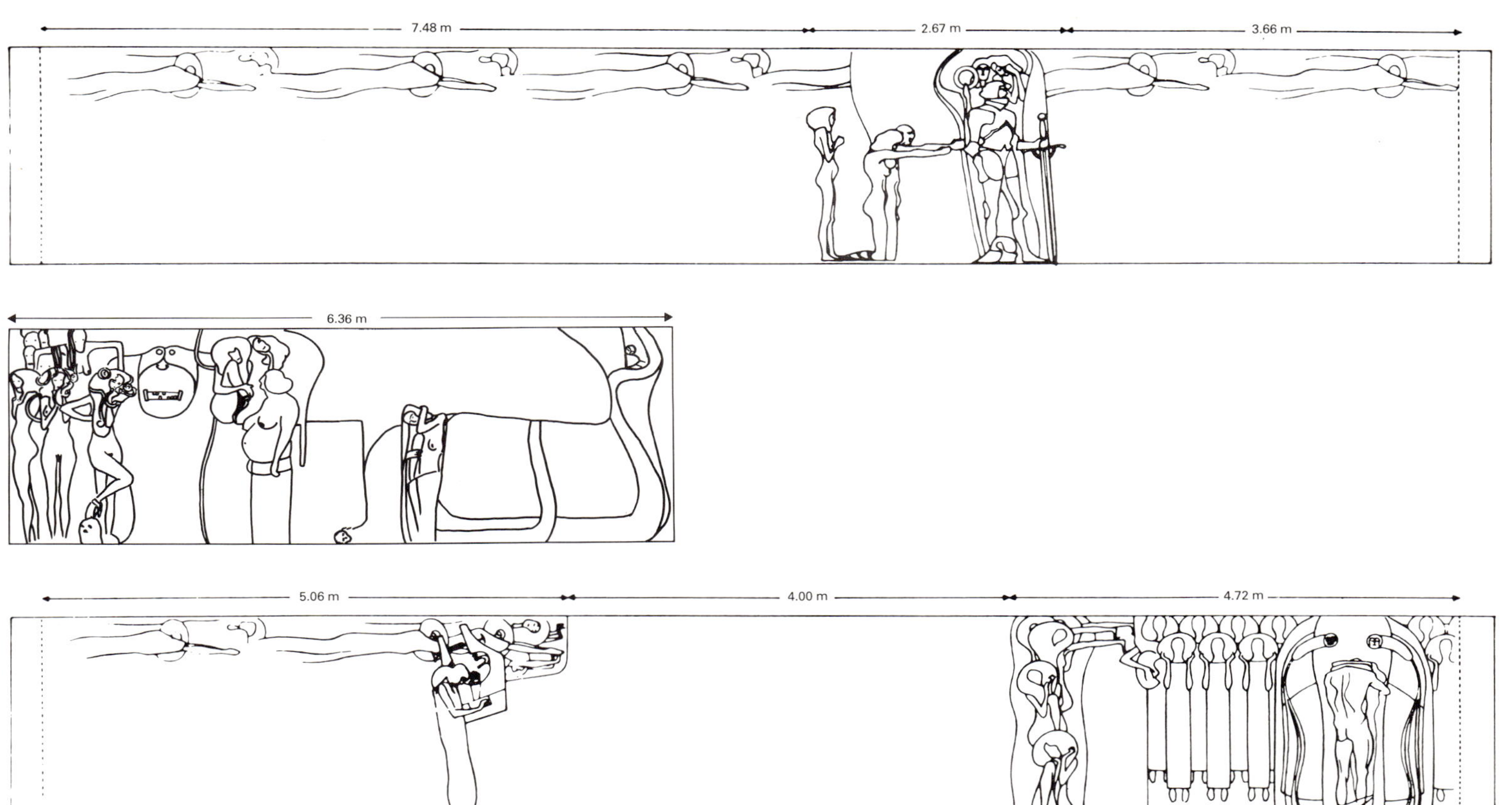

Overall sketch-plan of the Klimt Room: left, centre and right walls, with length indicated in metres.

the exception of the extreme right where "the longings and desires of mankind which fly above and beyond them" reappear; the giant Typhon, a monstrous ape with wings and a serpent's tail, and a formidable adversary of the Gods: to the left the three Gorgons, presented here as his daughters, and "Sickness, Madness and Death" which can only apply to the figures lurking behind the Gorgon, although there are more of them than can be identified from the catalogue; to the right, "Lust and Lewdness, Excess" (*Wollust und Unkeuschheit, Unmässigkeit*) designated in a different order by the three women in the centre of the panel; and lastly, still further to the right, "Nagging Care" (*Nagender Kummer*), an isolated female figure in front of the monster's tail. The third panel also has a title which may apply to the whole or only to its first part: "Longing for Happiness finds Repose in Poetry." And after the empty space above the opening through which the Klinger can be seen: "The Arts lead us into the Kingdom of the Ideal, where alone we can find pure Joy, pure Happiness, pure Love." "Choir of Heavenly

Angels." "Joy, Beautiful Divine Spark" (*Freude, schöner Götterfunke*). "This Kiss for the Whole World" (*Diesen Kuss der ganzen Welt*).

These two final phrases in inverted commas, which certainly refer to the last figures, are taken from Schiller's *Ode to Joy* (first and second lines of the penultimate stanza) as set to music at the end of the Ninth Symphony. This is an explicit invitation to read the whole program and layout as a transposition of that work. In fact, it has been possible to establish an exact and convincing parallel with the commentary on it by Wagner, one of its most famous exegetists, not only in his essay on Beethoven published in 1870, but in the program, less well known today, which he drafted in 1846 for the famous performance of the work at Dresden that marked the veritable resurrection of the score (text republished in 1871 in volume II of Wagner's complete writings).

Indeed Wagner presents the first movement from the beginning as "A struggle, in the most magnificent sense of the word, of the soul fighting for happiness against the oppression of that hostile power who interposes himself between us and earthly happiness" (*Ein Kampf der nach Freude ringenden Seele gegen den Druck jener feindlichen Gewalt, die sich zwischen uns und das Glück der Erde stellt*), which already seems to define the whole content of the three panels in very similar terms. "A male energy of resistance" (*Eine männliche Energie des Widerstandes*), which clearly seems to refer to the Knight in Armour, appears "opposite this formidable enemy" in the first movement, and on the first wall. In the second movement, the quotations from Goethe's *Faust* which Wagner calls on to suggest *false* joy, "delirium" (*Taumel*) and the "painful pleasures" (*schmerzlichen Genuss*) of the *molto vivace*, in which "Pain and Delight, Pleasure and Sorrow" are inextricably mingled, evoke very accurately some of the female figures in the second panel. The floating figures on the extreme right obviously seem to be equated with the "tireless instinct which drives us on with the energy of despair in search of happiness" that Wagner thought he could make out at the end of the movement, whereas the adagio that follows takes up the theme of repose. "Love and hope embrace to recover their gentle sway over our martyred heart." And *Faust* serves here to recall those "sweet celestial songs" (*süssen Himmelslieder*) whose music must be coming from the lyre of poetry. After the caesura in the frieze, we have the eruption of the final presto, which leads to the entrance of the choir with "Joy, Beautiful Divine Spark." Whereas Auchentaller takes up the same line in the poem to evoke the jubilation of the couples and Andri illustrates the central struggle, Klimt evokes Elysium, the "Kingdom of the Ideal," sanctuary (*Heiligtum*) of Joy, and then the kiss of the penultimate verse, according to Wagner, that "cry of universal human love" (*allgemeine Menschenliebe*): "we embrace the World on our breast." Then on 15 April 1902 Mahler concluded with the last verse.

This detailed program, which Wagner meant to be merely a simple guide for the listener, but which actually corresponds to Beethoven's main intentions (if we refer to his notes of 1823), presents a simple linear interpretation with transparent symbolism of both frieze and symphony. The longing for happiness for the good of all will only be satisfied in the realm of Joy after the triumph over the forces of Evil.

For Wagner in 1846 the brave decision to conduct this difficult work, which still had a mixed critical reception, was among other things, as he related in his autobiography *Mein Leben*, an attempt to reply "to a desperate question-mark facing my fate and my future... In the presence of this symphony the despair I tried to hide from my friends was transformed into enthusiasm." In Vienna, where the Ninth Symphony was created in 1824, but where recognition was more difficult than in Germany, it became the symbol of avant-garde struggles. Mahler, whose appointment as conductor of the Vienna Opera (and from 1897 as its director) was hotly disputed, had been given a lukewarm reception, by the critics at least, for his last interpretation on 22 January 1901. The hero's struggle against the hostile powers was an obvious projection of the artistic struggles of Beethoven, Wagner, Mahler and Klimt.

Yet the significance of the Ninth Symphony as a whole changed with the advent of different political and cultural contexts, transcending individual destinies. In Dresden in 1846 the lines of the *Ode to Joy* preserved and actually accentuated the progressive, even revolutionary meaning they had originally. In 1848, on the barricades at Dresden in front of the blazing Opera House, an insurgent shouted to Wagner: "Herr Kapellmeister, *Joy, Beautiful Divine Spark* set fire to it!" After the setback in '48 and progressively during the second half of the century, the "revolution" was increasingly concerned with the realm of art alone. In this respect, Carl E. Schorske has pertinently drawn attention to a poem by Ferdinand von Saar which, in 1891, gave eloquent testimony to the shift in meaning that was taking place. In Saar's *Kontraste* the weary workers repaving a street in Vienna are indifferent to the choral society of the school of operatic art which is rehearsing the *Ode to Joy*. "Embrace, you millions!" (*Seid umschlungen Millionen!*) and "All men become brothers" (*Alle Menschen werden Brüder*) are words which no longer penetrate their consciousness. Henceforth they are reserved for the concert hall. Nor are they the words that Mahler and Klimt retained in 1902. After the social aspirations of Art Nouveau in its early days and even of the Secession in 1897, Joy is reserved for the hero alone and the "millions" are simply invited to prostrate themselves before the Creator. Betrayed by Utopia, Saar committed suicide in 1906.

Wagner and his music continued to play an ambiguous role in Vienna. The composer's nationalism had been ill received by the rationality of the German liberals. And Eduard Hanslick, now a determined opponent, tried to be obstructive at the bar of the *Neue Freie Presse* by attacking, to give an example, "the absence of form laid down as a principle" which he thought he observed in *Tristan* (1891). For the younger generation, on the other hand, in the only cultural field in which they now carried on their struggle, Wagner became the rallying point for the modernists, in spite of the Pan-Germanist and anti-Semitic connotations in his work and actions which served to lend support to the right. Hartel, the Minister of Culture in Körber's government, was himself a fervent Wagnerian, but also a fierce opponent of the anti-Semitism which still corroded Vienna. A combination which led quite naturally but highly symbolically to the historic performances of *Tristan* at the Opera in February 1903, with Mahler as conductor and Alfred Roller, chairman of the organizing committee of the Beethoven exhibition of 1902, as stage designer.

This entente, however, could only be effected by a complete "transfer" of the "form" of the work, independently of its ideological content. The concept of the total work of art to which Klinger paid dual homage by his own *Beethoven* and more directly by the last sentences of his text of 1891 reproduced in the 1902 catalogue, which quotes Wagner, also does much to meet the new aspirations of the Viennese avant-garde of Art Nouveau.

Liberation and sublimation by art alone: that has become the primary meaning of the Ninth Symphony, in the interpretation of it now put forward by the frieze. In this sense, it goes further than the contemporary interpretations of Bourdelle or Romain Rolland, who simply ended his *Life of Beethoven* of 1902 with the composer's famous slogan (taken from a letter of 1815 to Countess Erdödy): "Joy through Suffering" (*Durch Leiden Freude*). In the autumn of 1902, the last section of the frieze was incorporated into the Klimt retrospective (eighteenth Secession exhibition) under the title "My Kingdom is not of this World" (*Mein Reich ist nicht von dieser Erde*). The biblical phrase which the painter henceforth took for his motto now refers back to Wagner's 1870 essay, which summed up the interpretation the composer then proposed of the Ninth Symphony and its redeeming music in the midst of a corrupt civilization: "Just as under the world-civilization of the Romans Christianity emerged, music now emerges amidst the chaos of modern civilization. Both say to us: 'Our kingdom is not of this world.' That means, we come from within, you from without; we derive from the essence of things, you merely from their appearance."

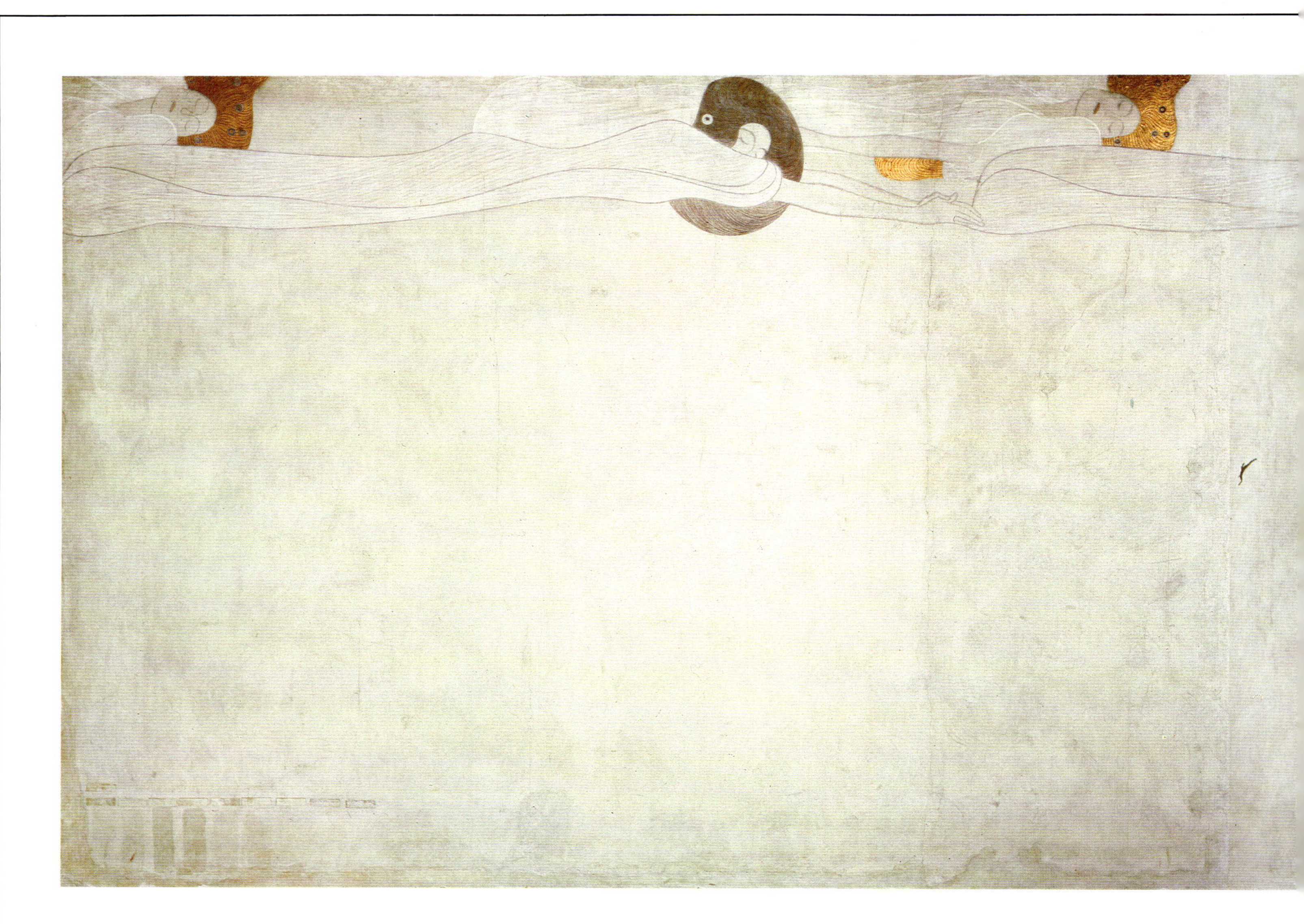

Gustav Klimt
Frieze for the Beethoven Exhibition of 1902.
Left panel: The Longing for Happiness (pages 30-33).
Overall length: 45 ft. 3 in.

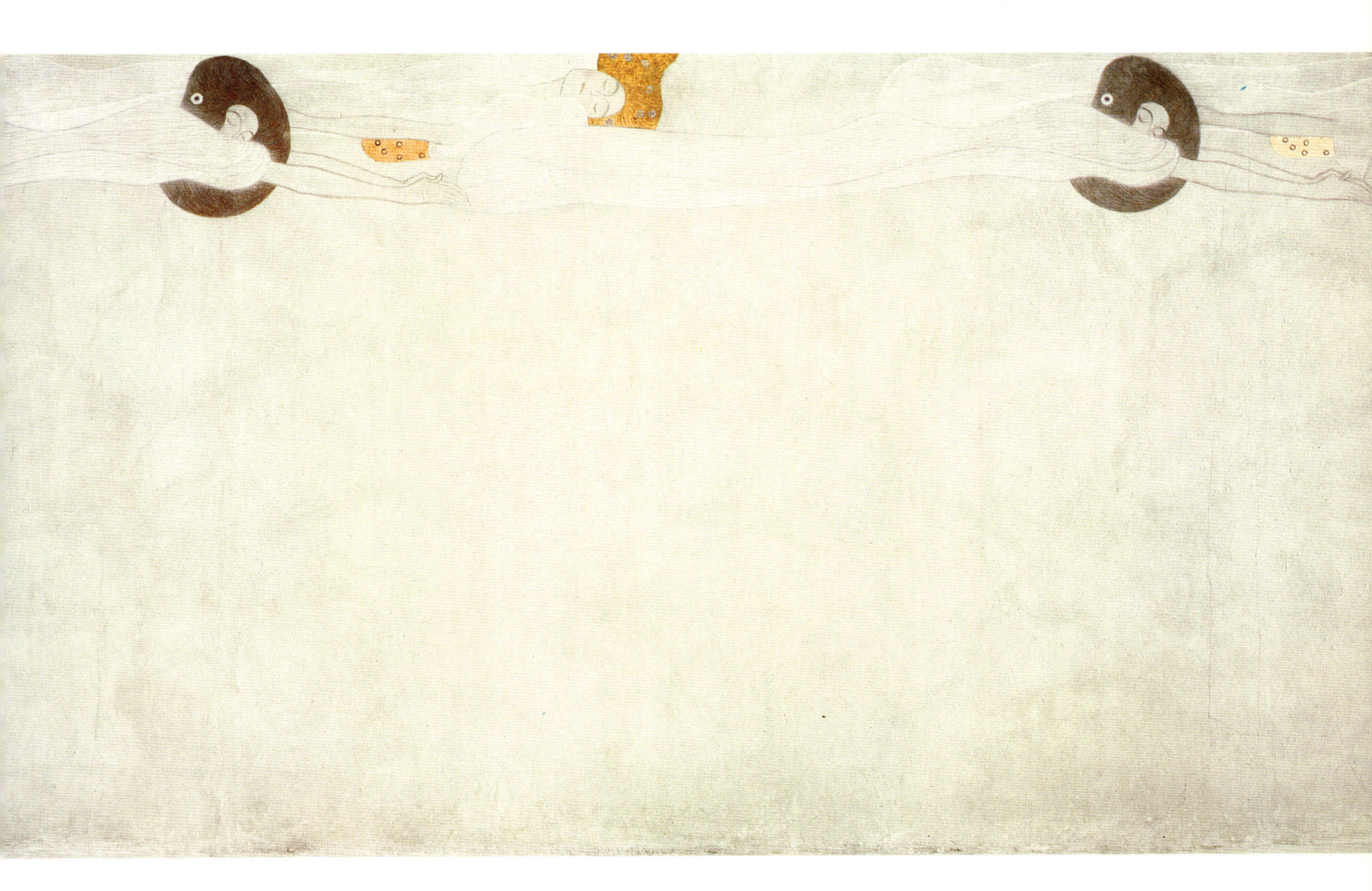

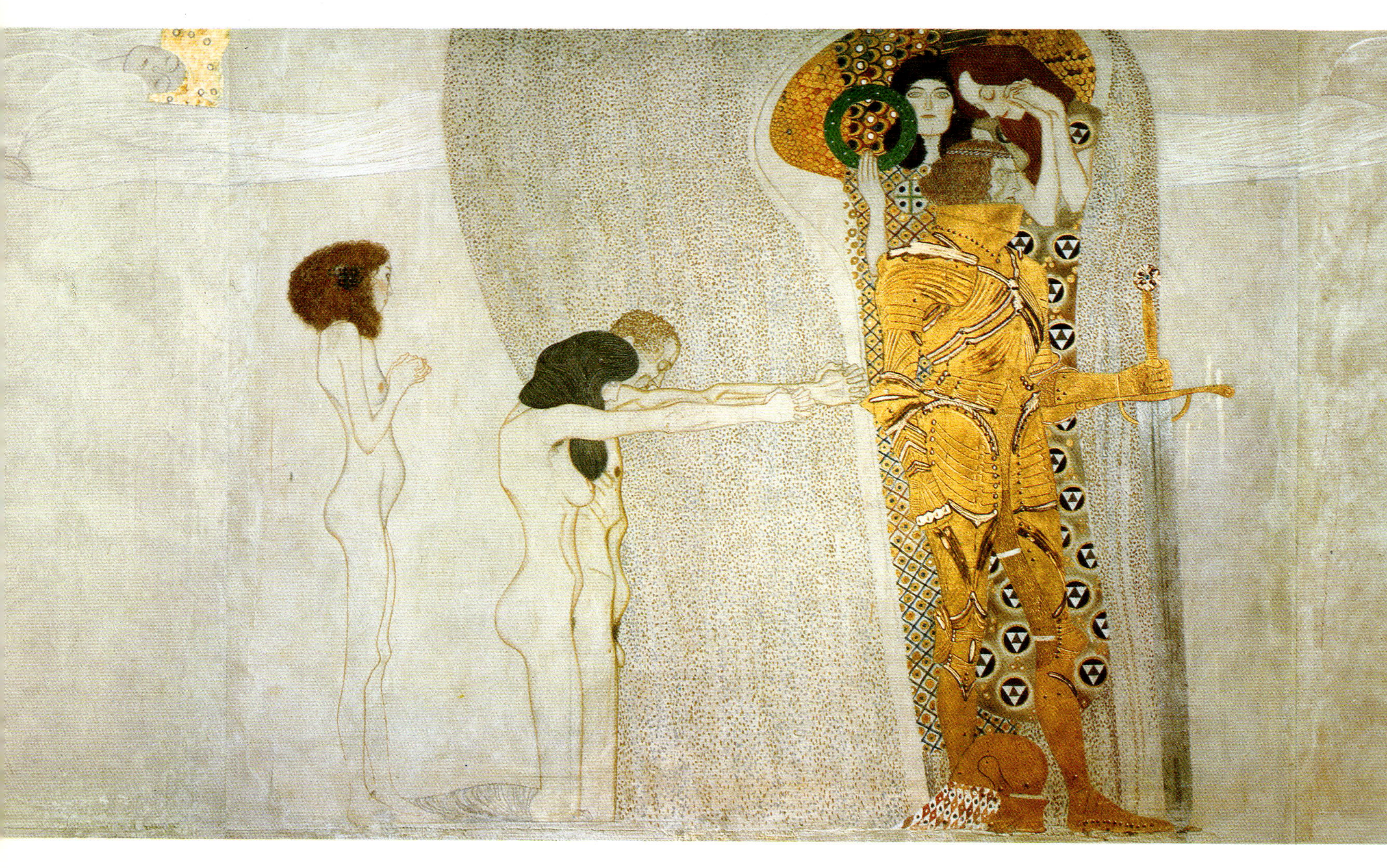

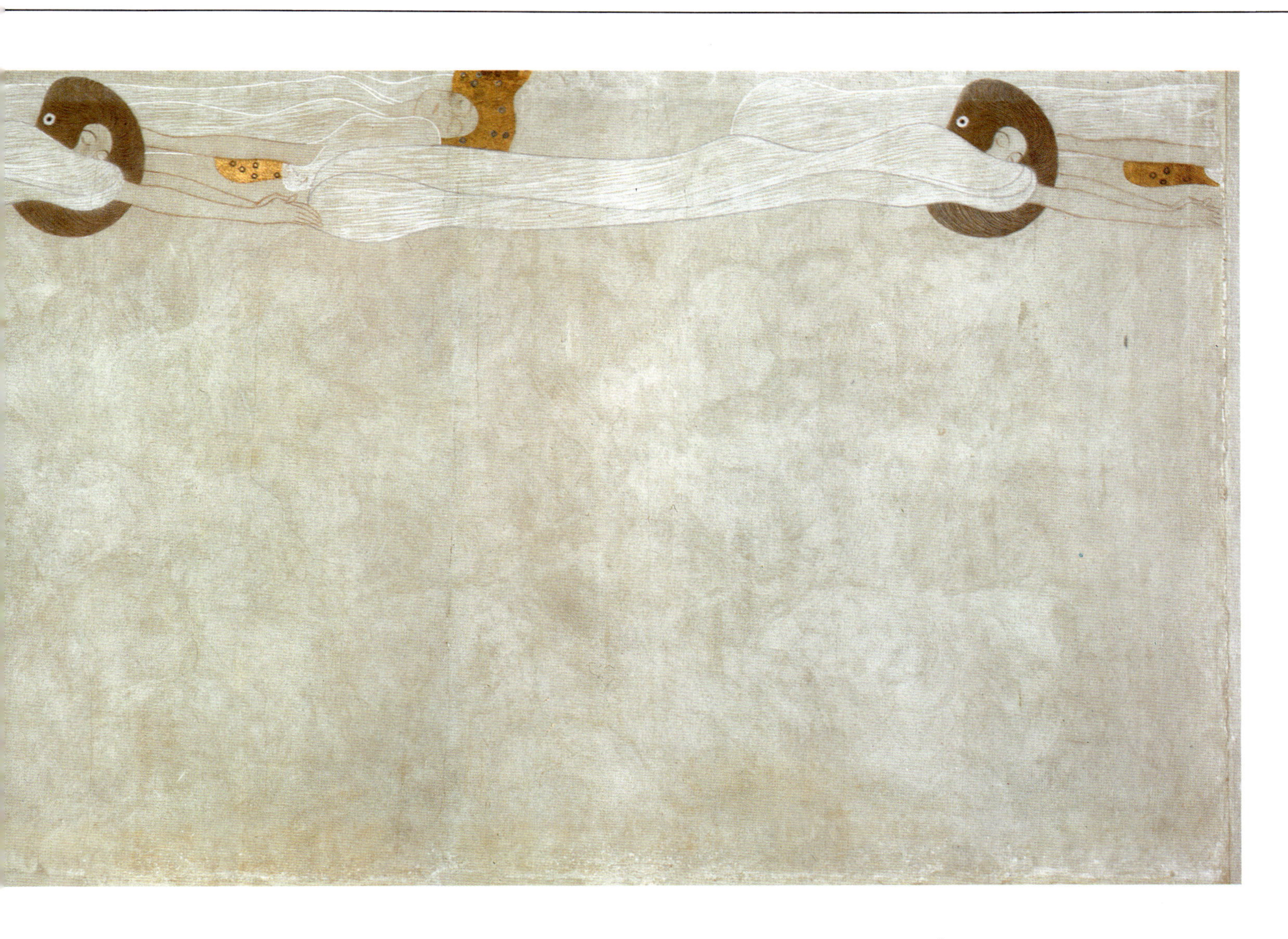

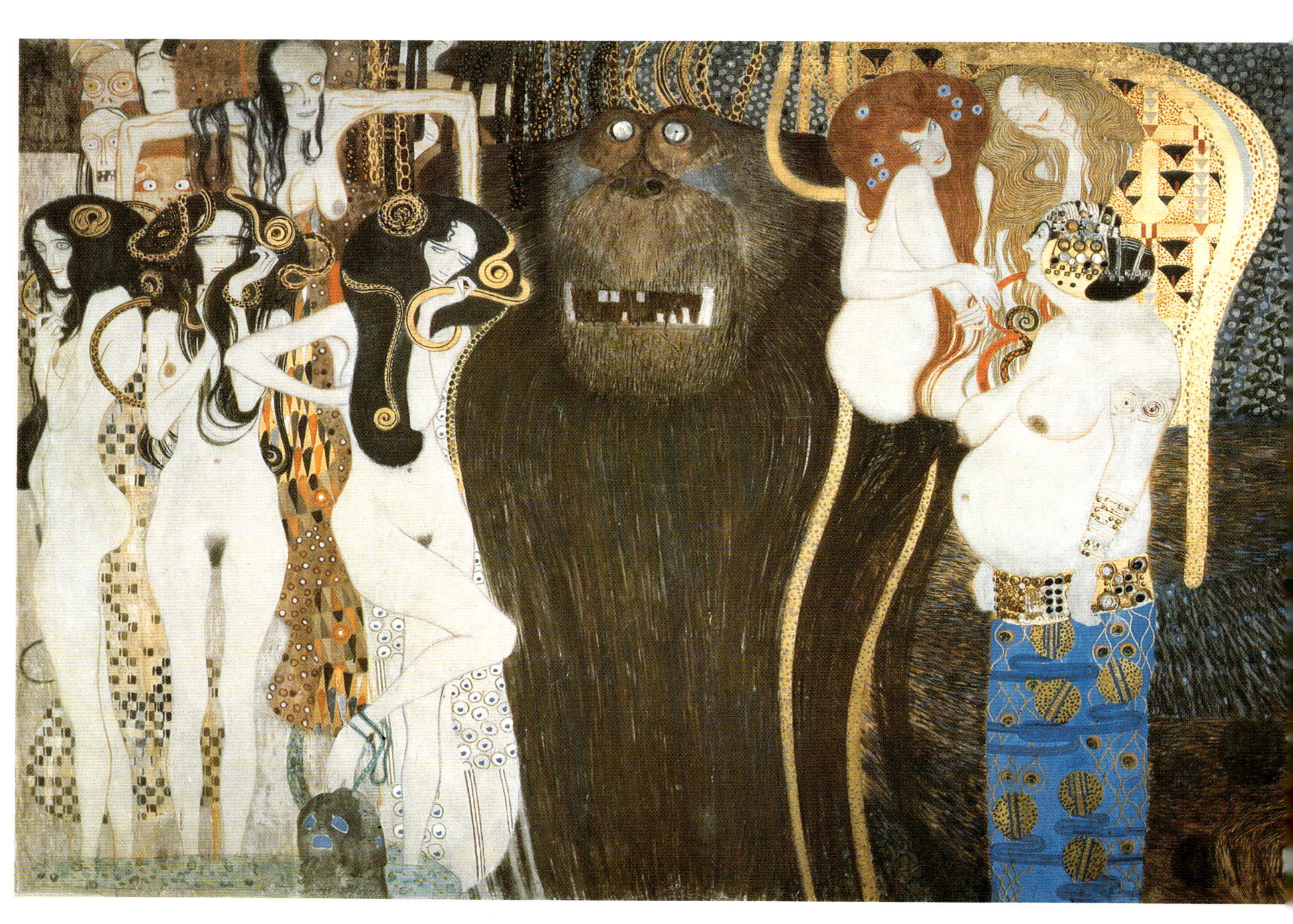

Gustav Klimt
Frieze for the Beethoven Exhibition of 1902.
Central panel: The Hostile Powers (pages 34-35)
Overall length: 20 ft. 10 in.

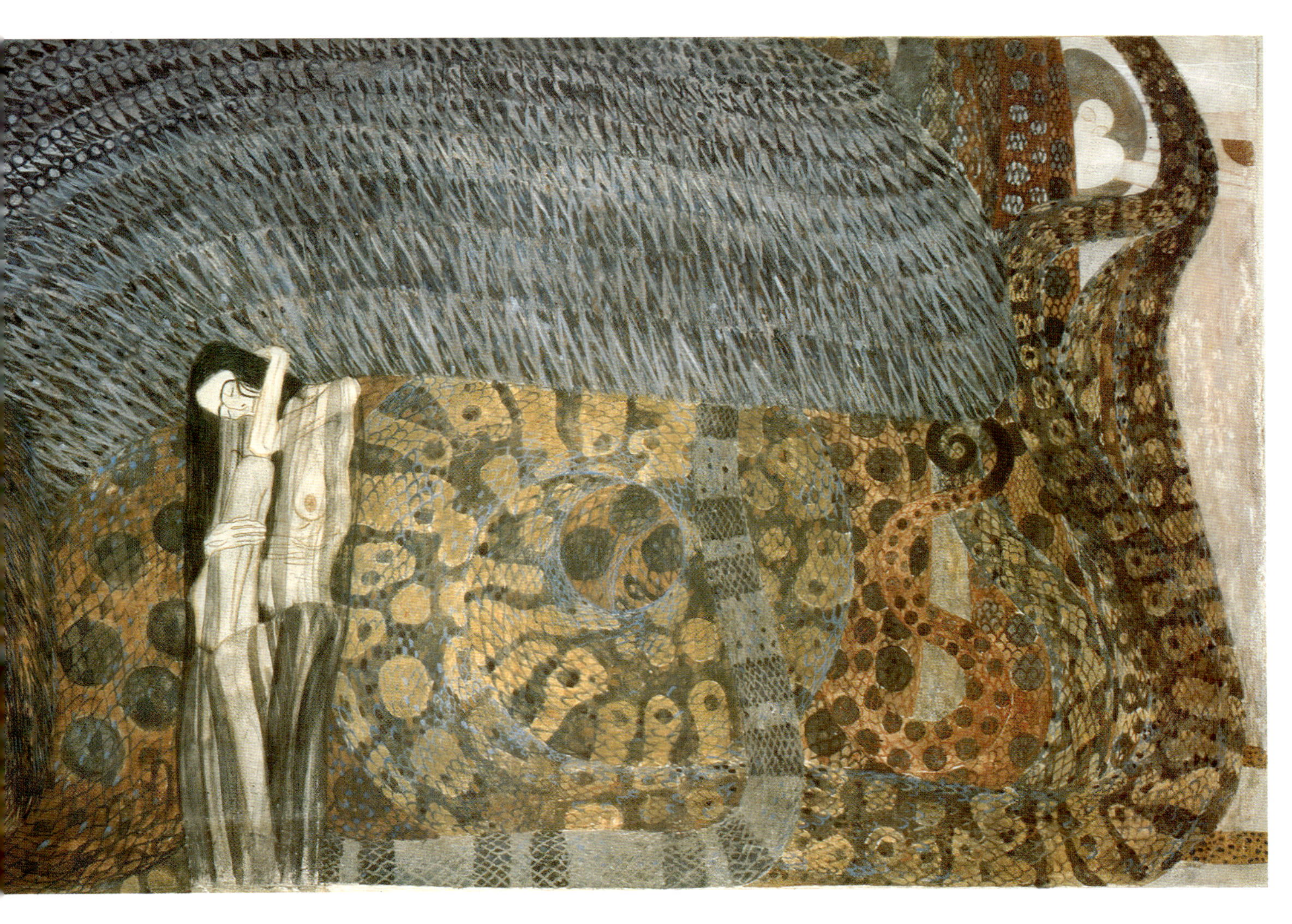

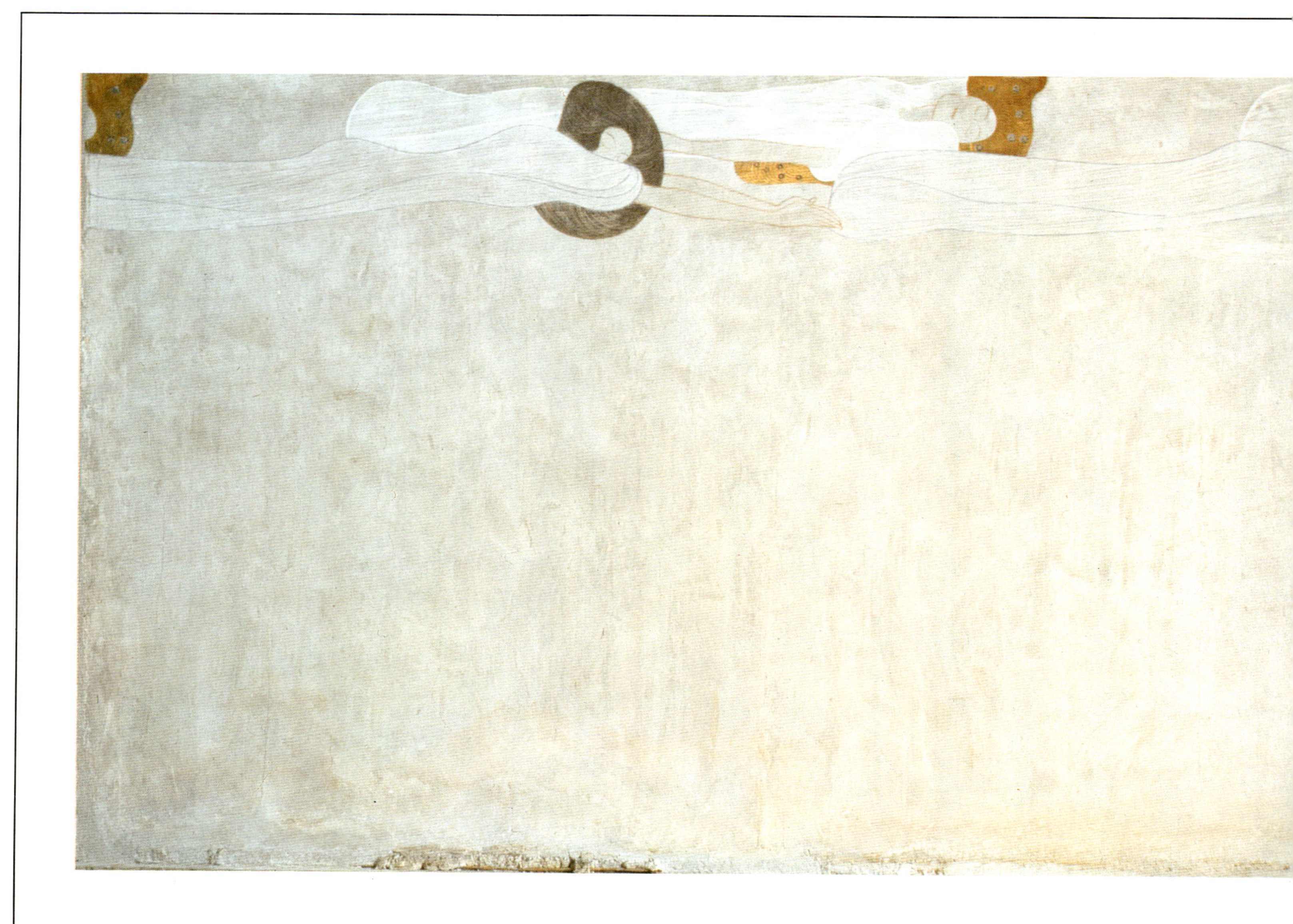

Gustav Klimt
Frieze for the Beethoven Exhibition of 1902.
Right panel: The Longing for Happiness finds Repose in Poetry (pages 36-39).
Overall length: 16 ft. 9 in. + 13 ft. 1 in. unpainted + 15 ft. 5 in.

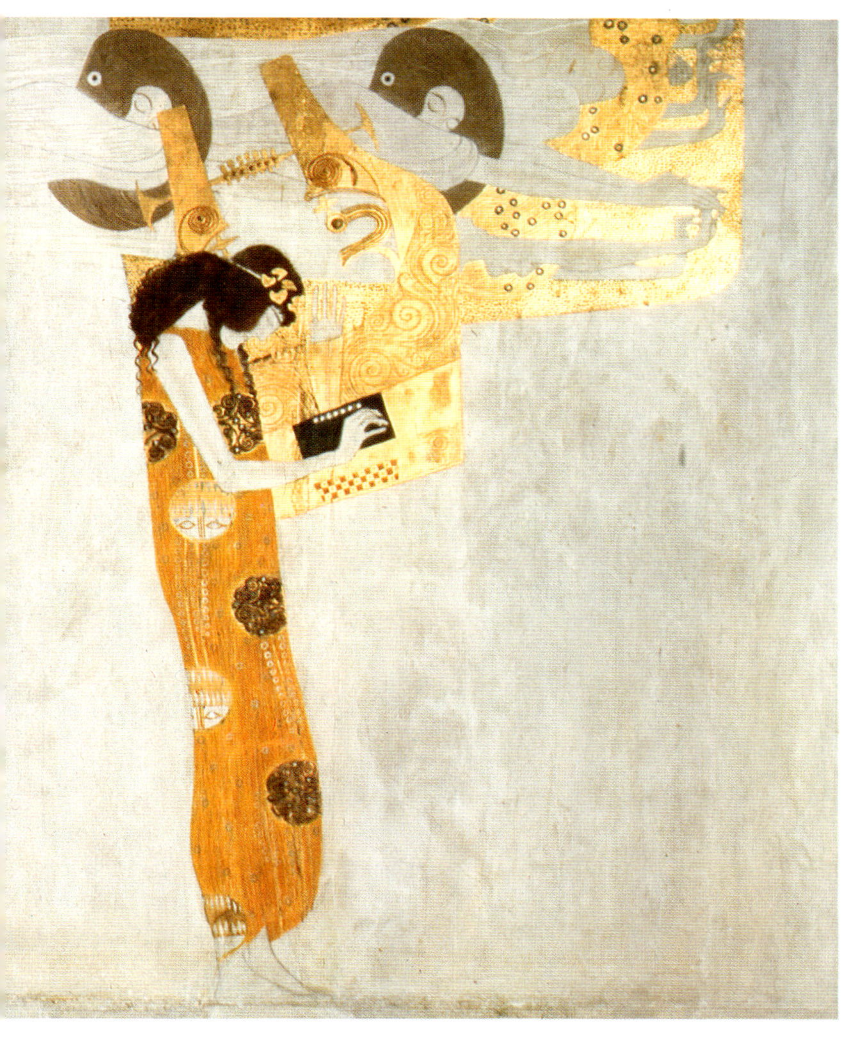

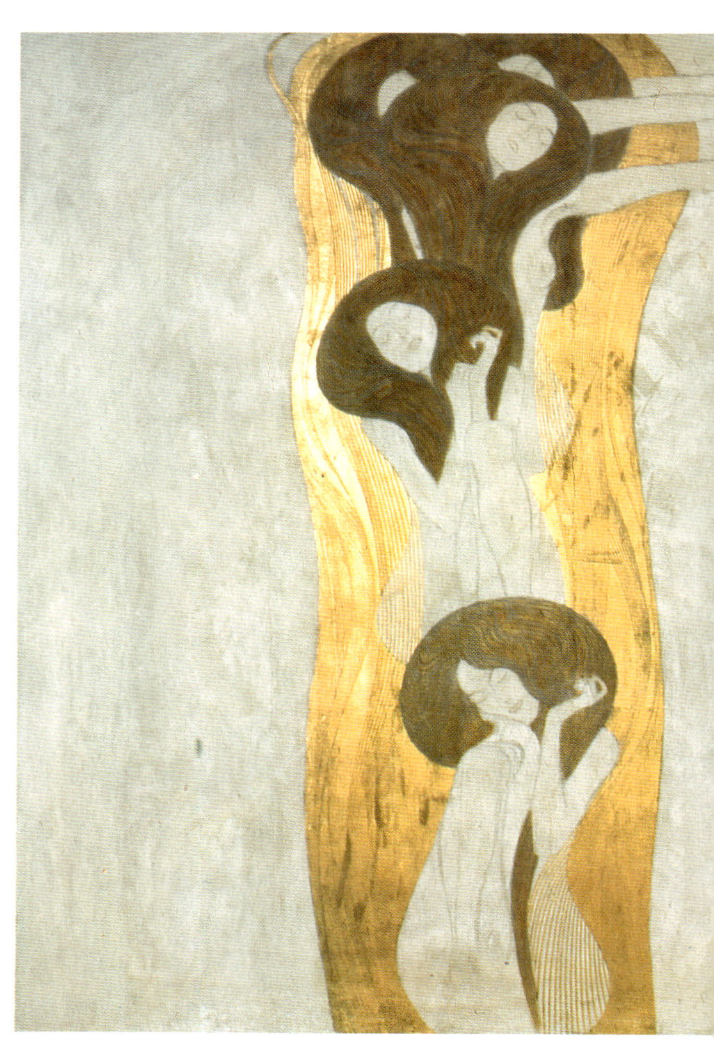

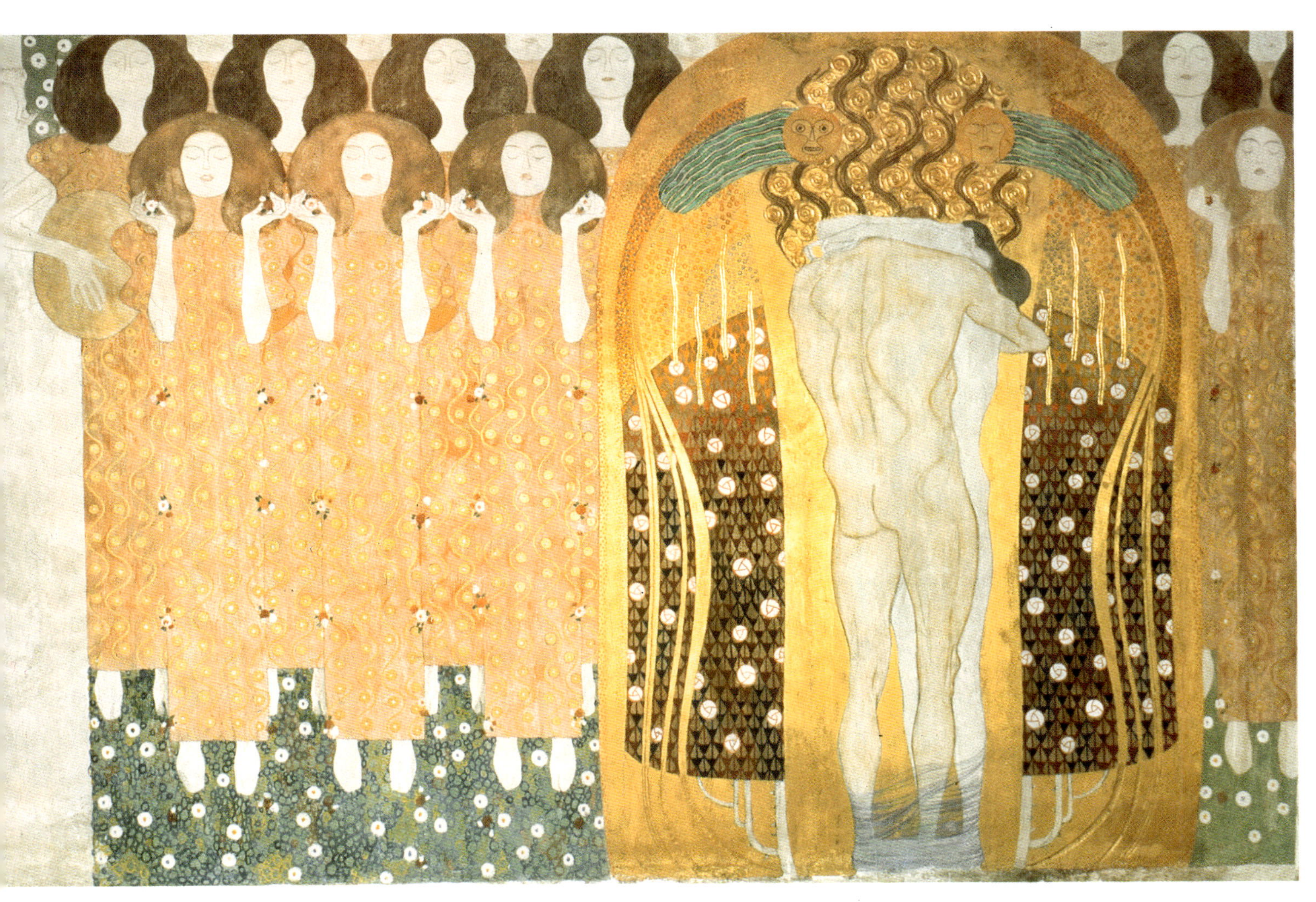

Left panel: The Floating Figures.

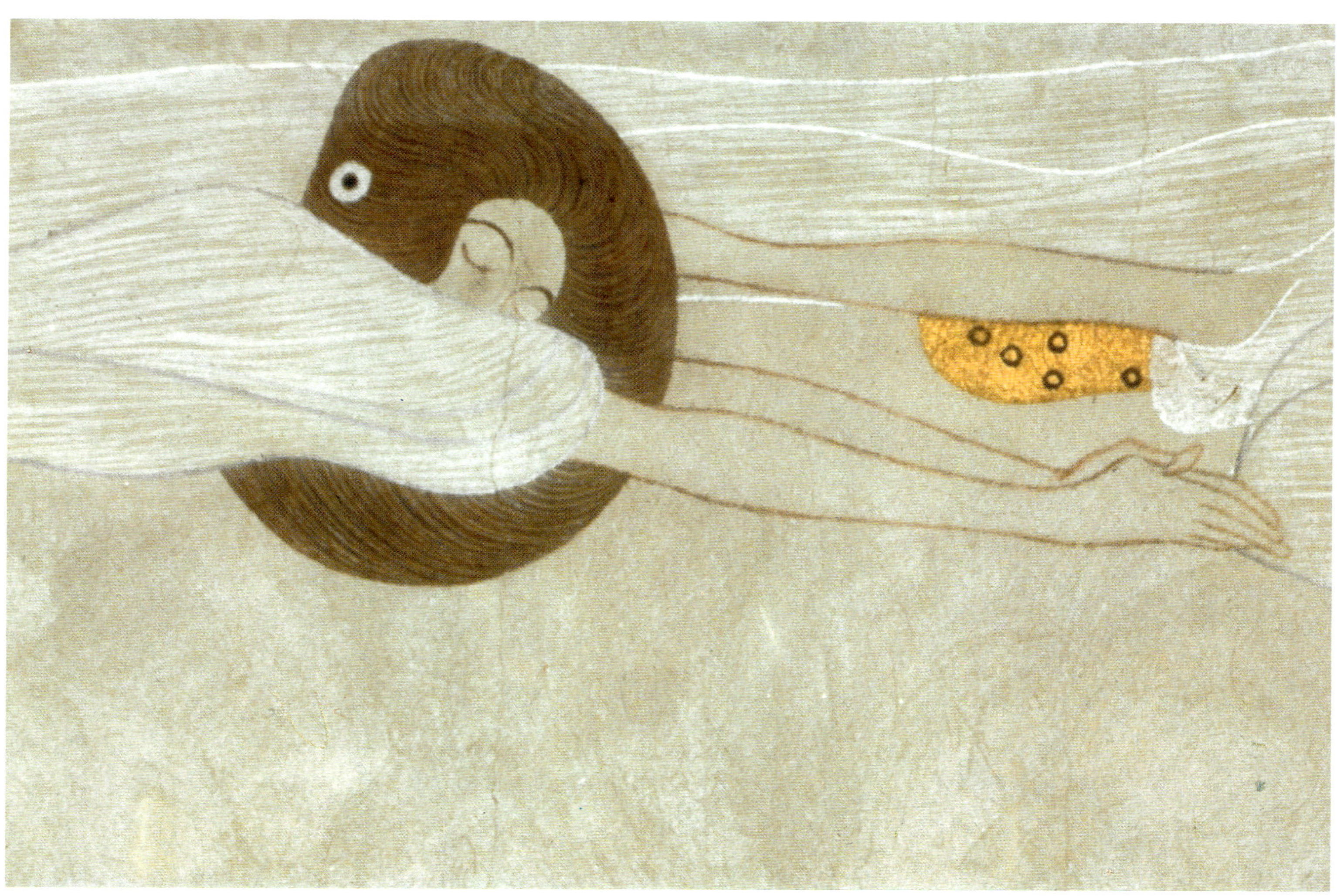

IV
Iconography

NEVERTHELESS, this linear interpretation is not quite complete, even at the simple level of iconography. The precise motifs chosen by Klimt to illustrate this program carry with them a whole procession of images which accompany and echo them, both in his own work and in that of the artists from whom he may have borrowed figures, subjects or images.

Everything begins with the interrogation of the World Mystery posed at the entrance by the floating figures. The motif, in which the essential mural quality conferred on it by Puvis de Chavannes forms an important transitional stage, had a long tradition, but Klimt

Right panel: The Floating Figures.

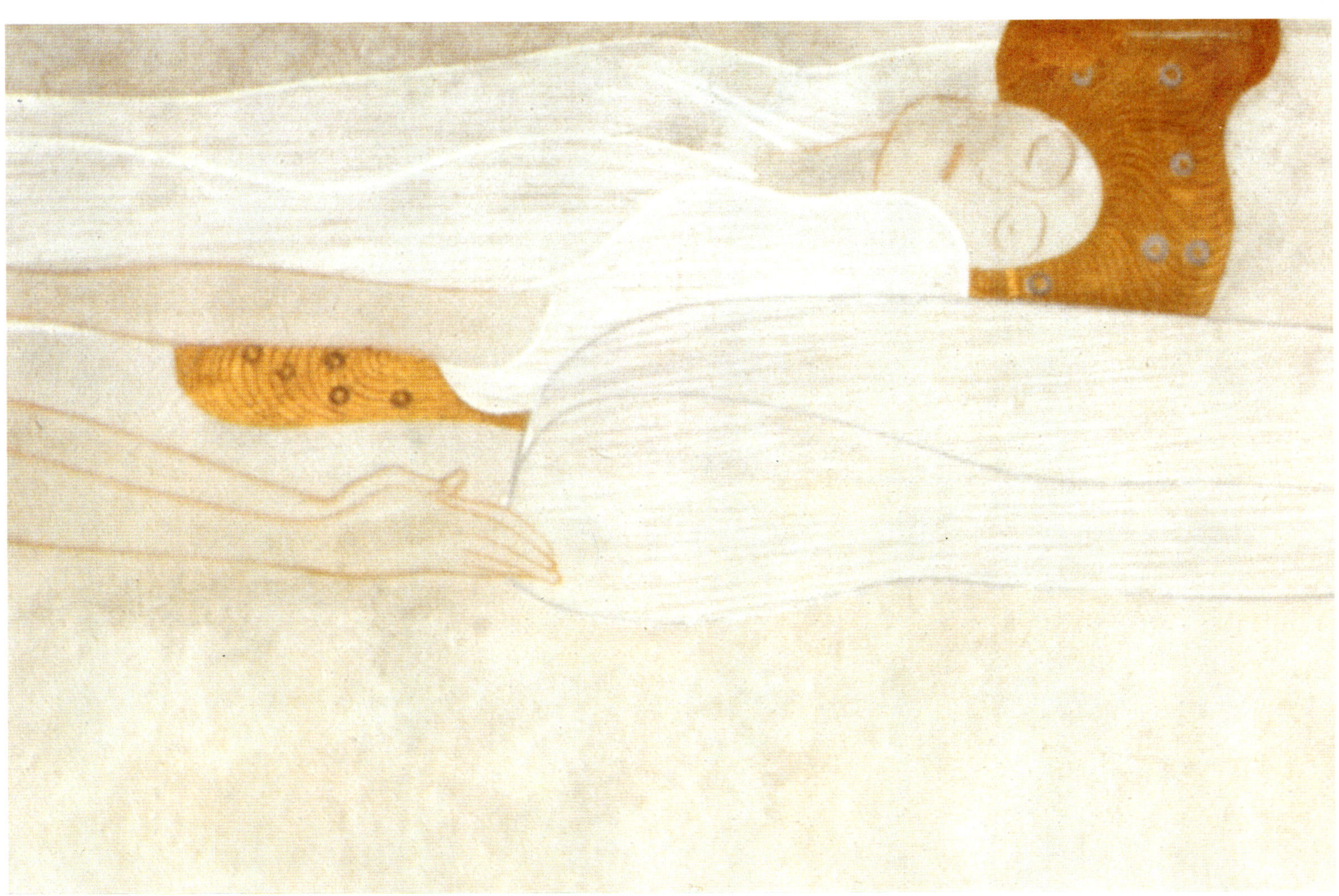

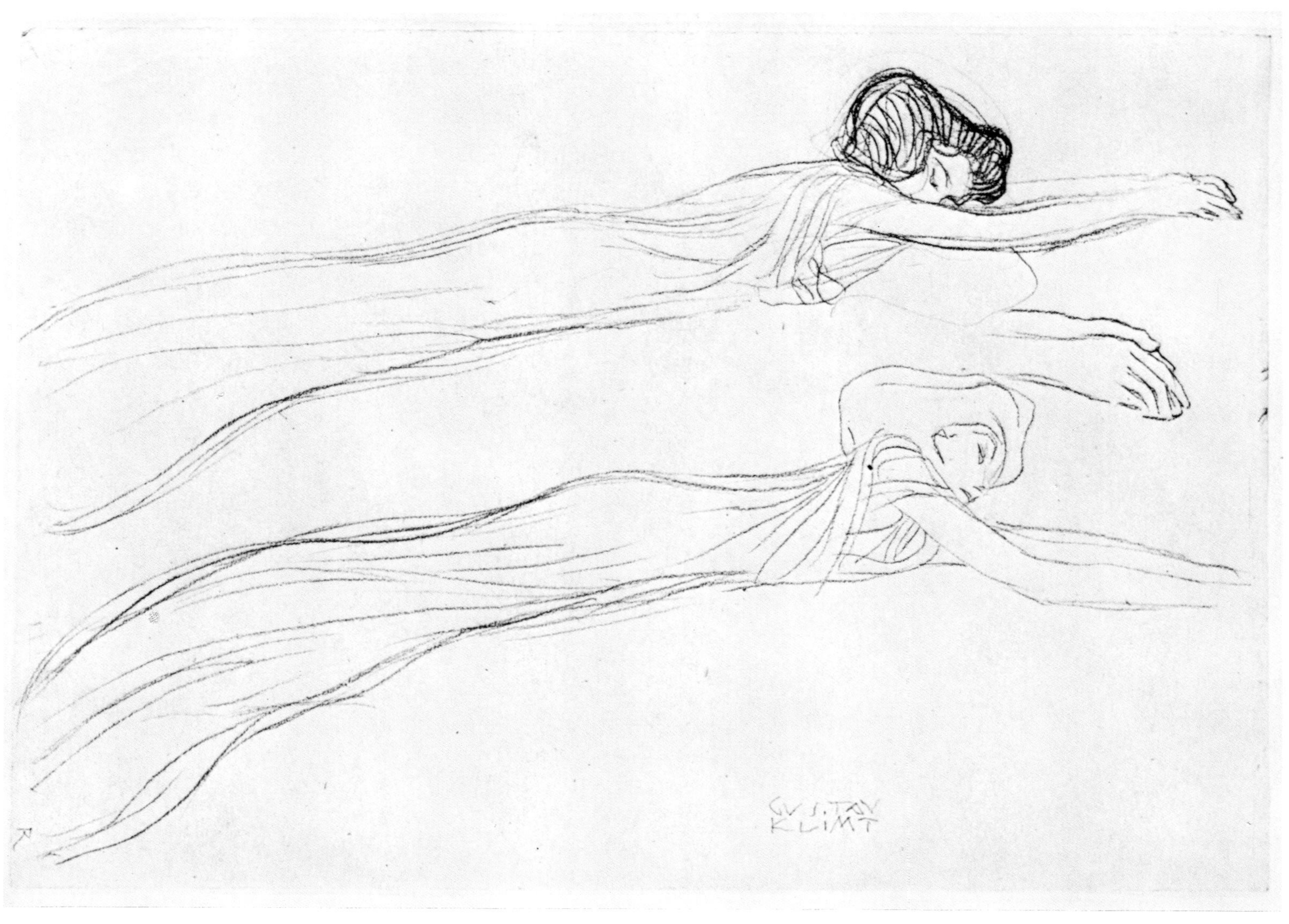

Gustav Klimt
Studies for the Floating Figures. Black chalk.

probably adopted it from the Dutch painter Jan Toorop, i.e. at the point in time when international Symbolism came to a halt, having run out of breath and forms. Toorop was well known in Vienna where his most celebrated works such as *The Three Brides*, *The Prowlers*, *Fatalism* and *The Garden of Sufferings* were familiar from reproductions in German periodicals and even more so from the actual Secession exhibitions in 1900 (seventh) and 1901 (twelfth). One of his most ambitious works, the *Sphinx* of 1892-1897, was shown in 1899 at the House of Artists, as has recently been proved. There is no doubt that Klimt, like the Viennese public, had taken a good look at Toorop's complicated drawings and hermetic figures. It is much more doubtful whether he tried to decipher their precise meaning, and still less extract their symbolism. But he did take from them the "figures" in the full sense of the word: a form signifying less by what it represents than by what it shows, for example the kneeling bodies and the imploring arms of suffering Humanity, the bridge to the Kingdom of the Ideal built by the outstretched arms of the Arts, or that Longing for Happiness which comes even more directly from Toorop's 1899 illustration in a Dutch book owned by a Viennese admirer of the painter, who was also a friend and patron of the Secession, Fritz Wärndorfer. But Klimt's preliminary study which ensures the transition also shows, by the search for rhythmic continuity and its highly Hodlerian parallelism which was to lead to the alternation of raised and lowered faces, how the rupture between a symbolist imagery still drifting in search of its form and the meaningful organization of surfaces which characterizes the real work of Art Nouveau painters is effected. In the faience and glass mosaic medallion set in the same wall, Kolo Moser gives an attenuated echo of it, impeded in this case by the resistence and static quality of a material unsuited to the design it is meant to bear.

Jan Toorop (1858-1928):
Illustration for Egedius en de vreemdeling
by W.G. van Nouhuys, Haarlem, 1899.

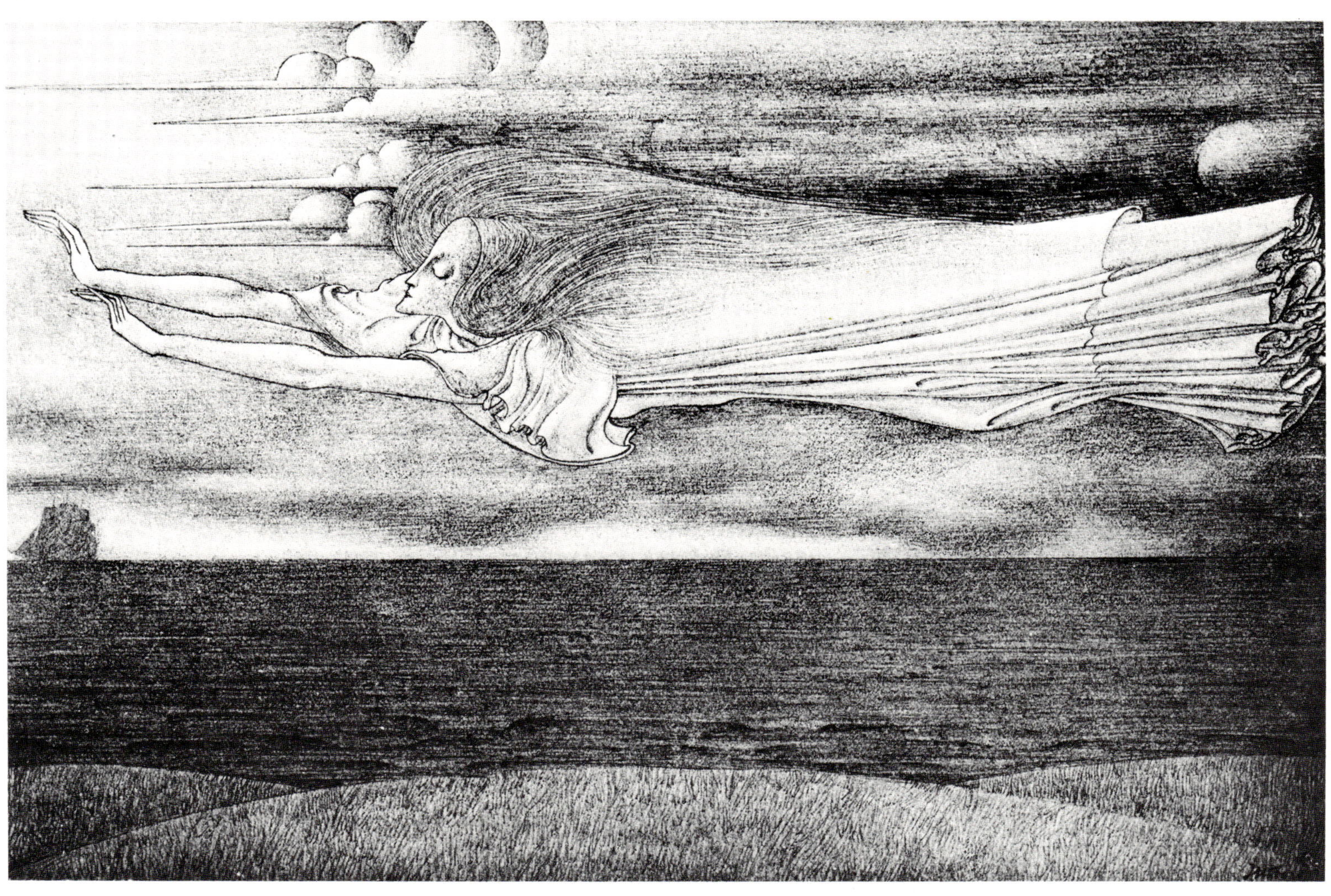

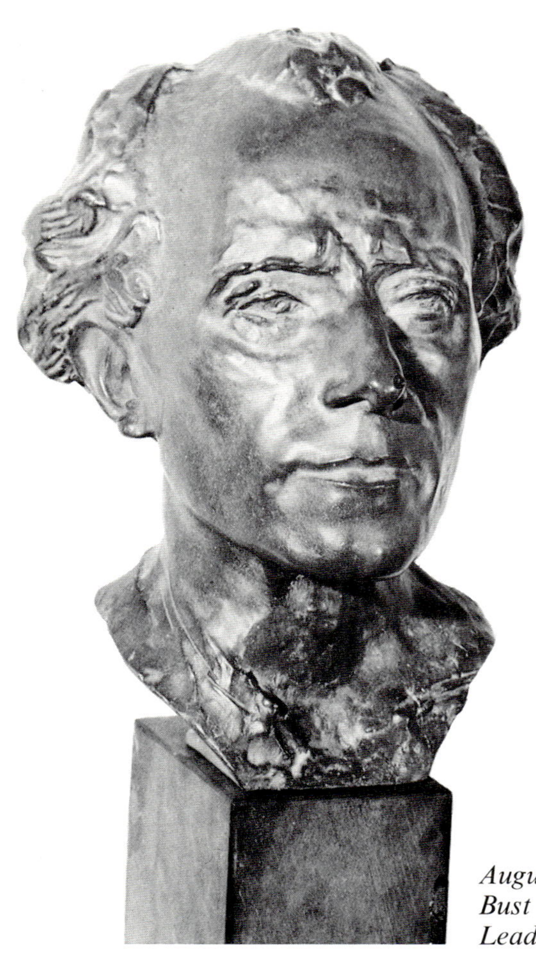

Auguste Rodin (1840-1917): Bust of Gustav Mahler, 1909. Lead.

Lorenz Helmschmied: Suit of armour for Archduke Siegmund of Tyrol, Augsburg, 1485.

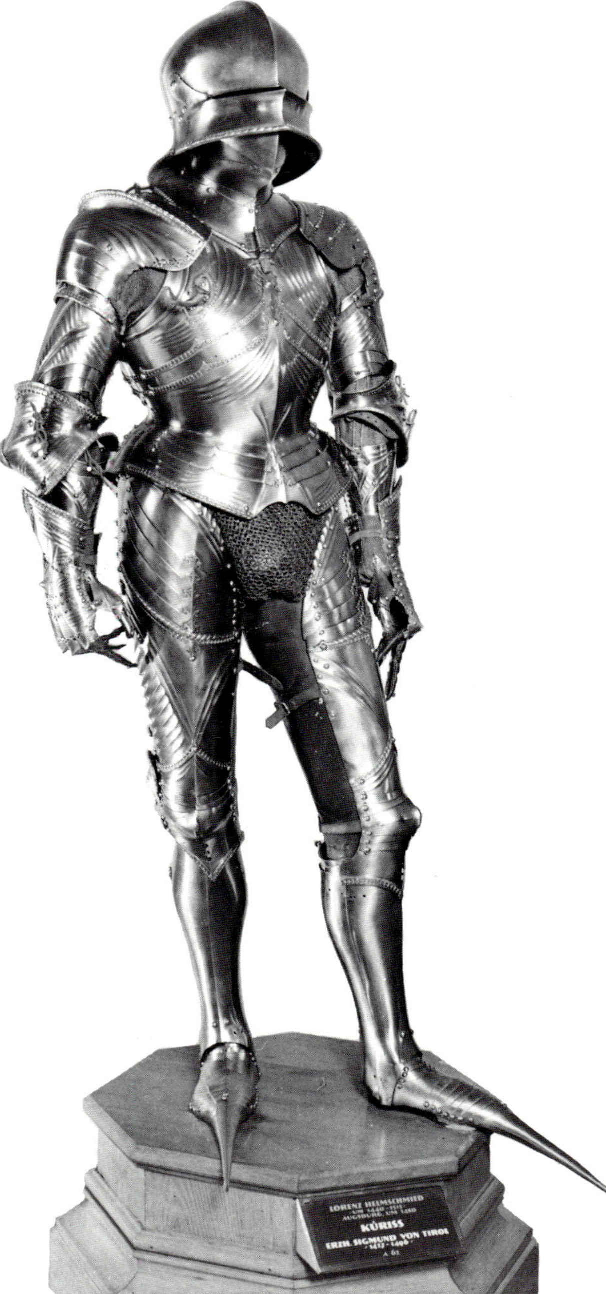

In the same way, the group of the Knight in Armour condenses and sums up an iconography which goes far beyond the strictly Beethoven-cum-Wagnerian program. In its Assyrio-Egyptian combination of frontality and strict profile we rediscover the double image of the Athene who helped Theseus in his struggle against the Minotaur of obscurantism on the poster for the first Secession exhibition and the Athene, who in the same year, 1898, showed the spectator the "naked truth" of Art Nouveau (as opposed to the historicist lie) in the place of the traditional Winged Victory. In 1902 the Medusa head common to both of them, grimacing provocatively at the public, emigrated to the neighbouring wall with the two other Gorgons. A figure fighting for Enlightenment, Athene now wears a suit of armour designed at Augsburg in the fifteenth century for Archduke Siegmund of Tyrol. Now she is the Wagnerian hero, another Siegfried, who has doffed her helmet (belonging to another panoply, but also borrowed from the collections in the Kunsthistorisches Museum) the better to bring out the similarity between her

Left panel: Group of the Knight in Armour, Ambition and Pity.

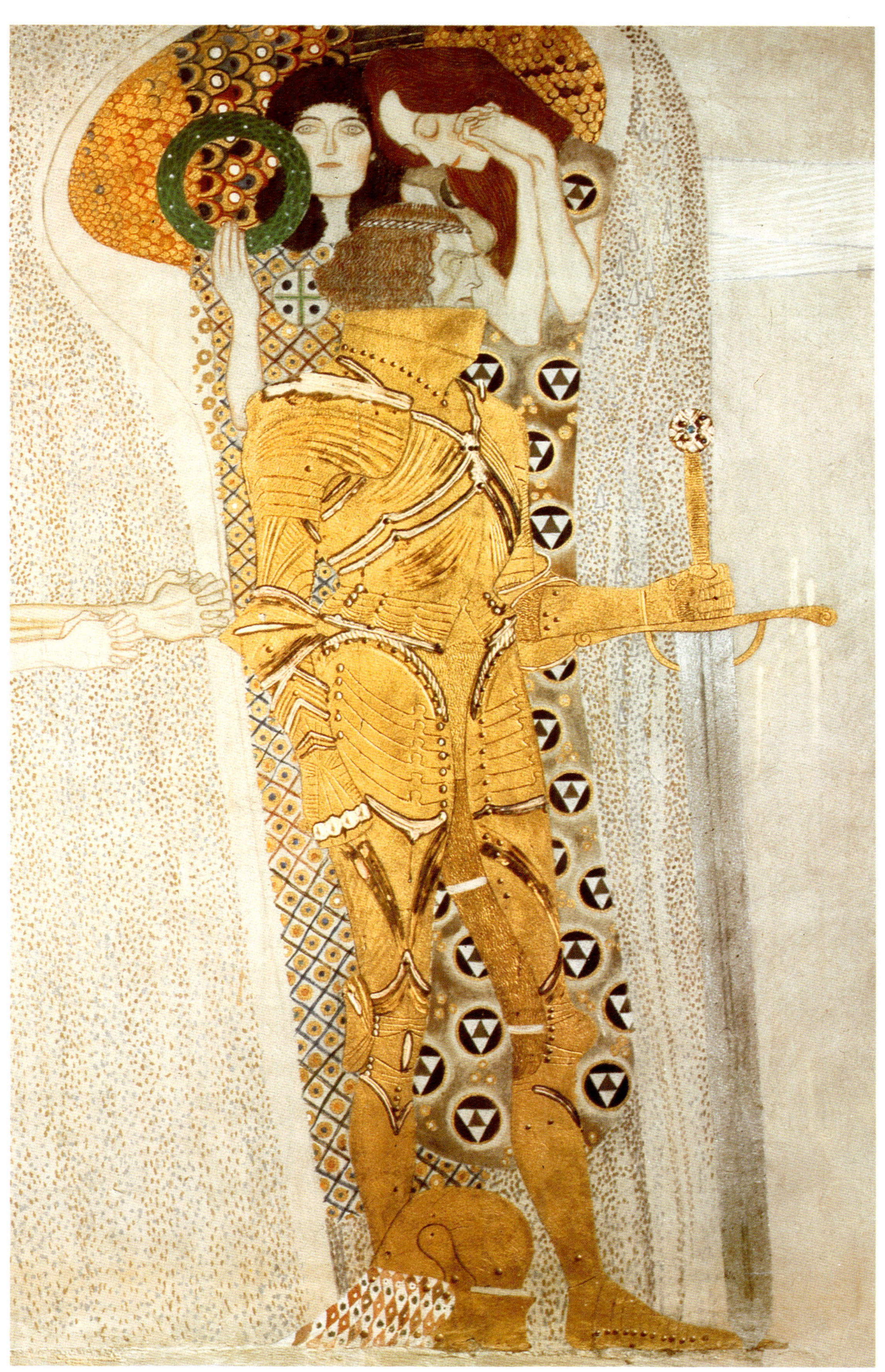

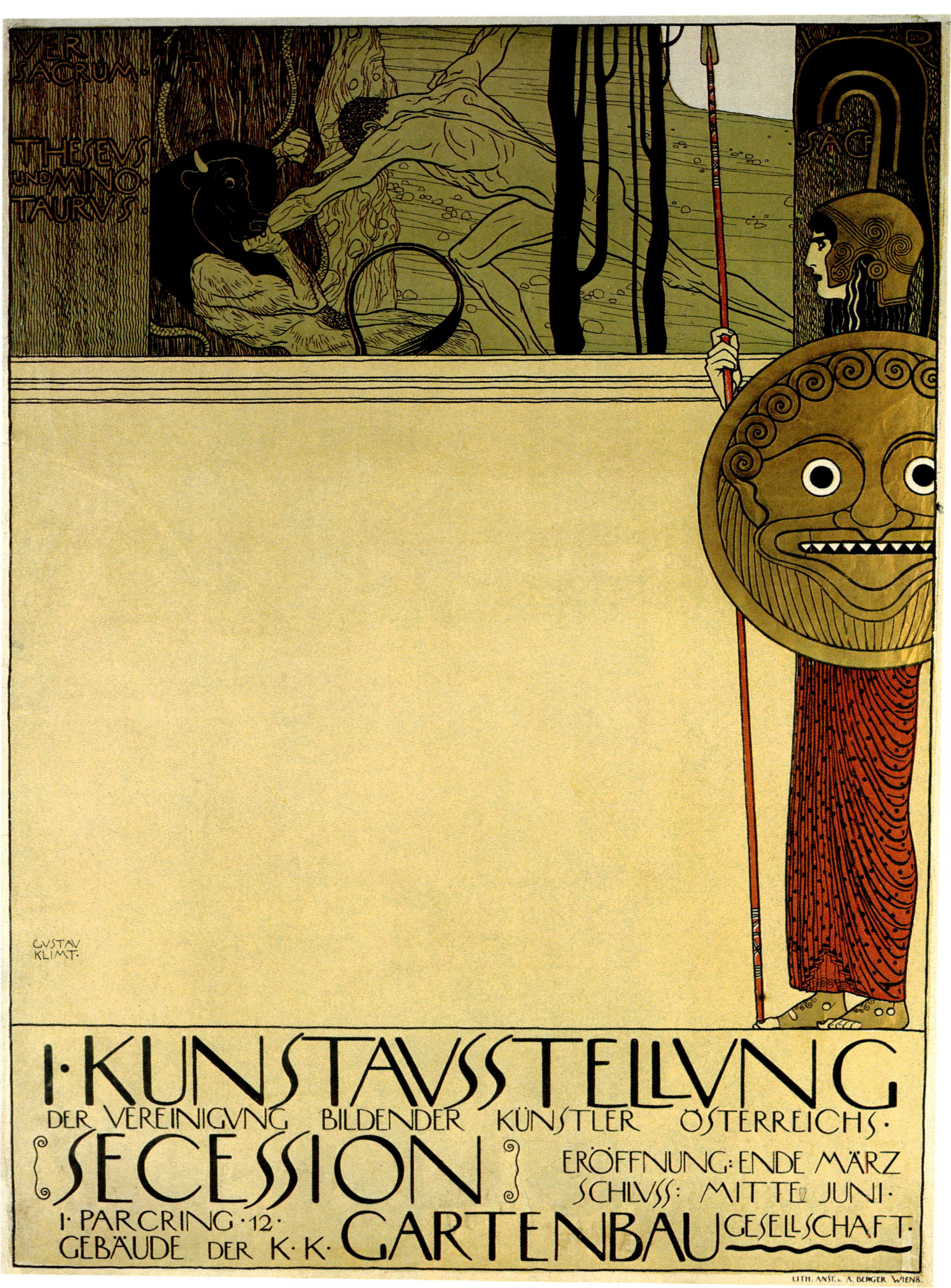

Gustav Klimt
Poster for the first exhibition of the Vienna Secession, 1898.
Above, Theseus and the Minotaur. Right, Pallas Athene.

face and Gustav Mahler's. And the similarity pointed out by contemporaries was confirmed in 1910 by Klimt himself when he chose this figure as his contribution to the Festschrift for Mahler published by the author Paul Stefan. Thanks to Wagner and Beethoven the two avant-gardes and their respective heralds had naturally come together.

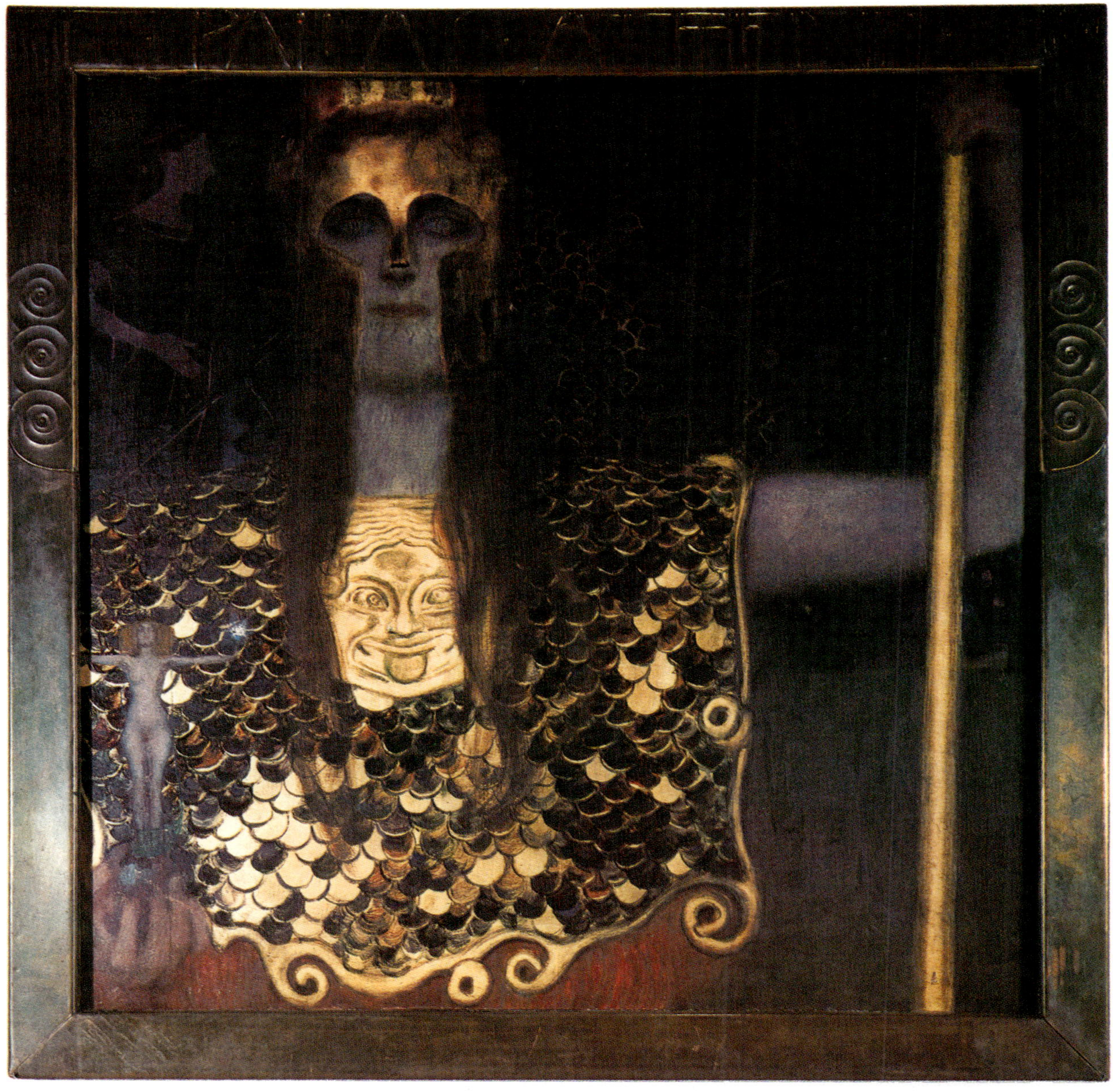

Gustav Klimt
Pallas Athene, 1898.
Oil.

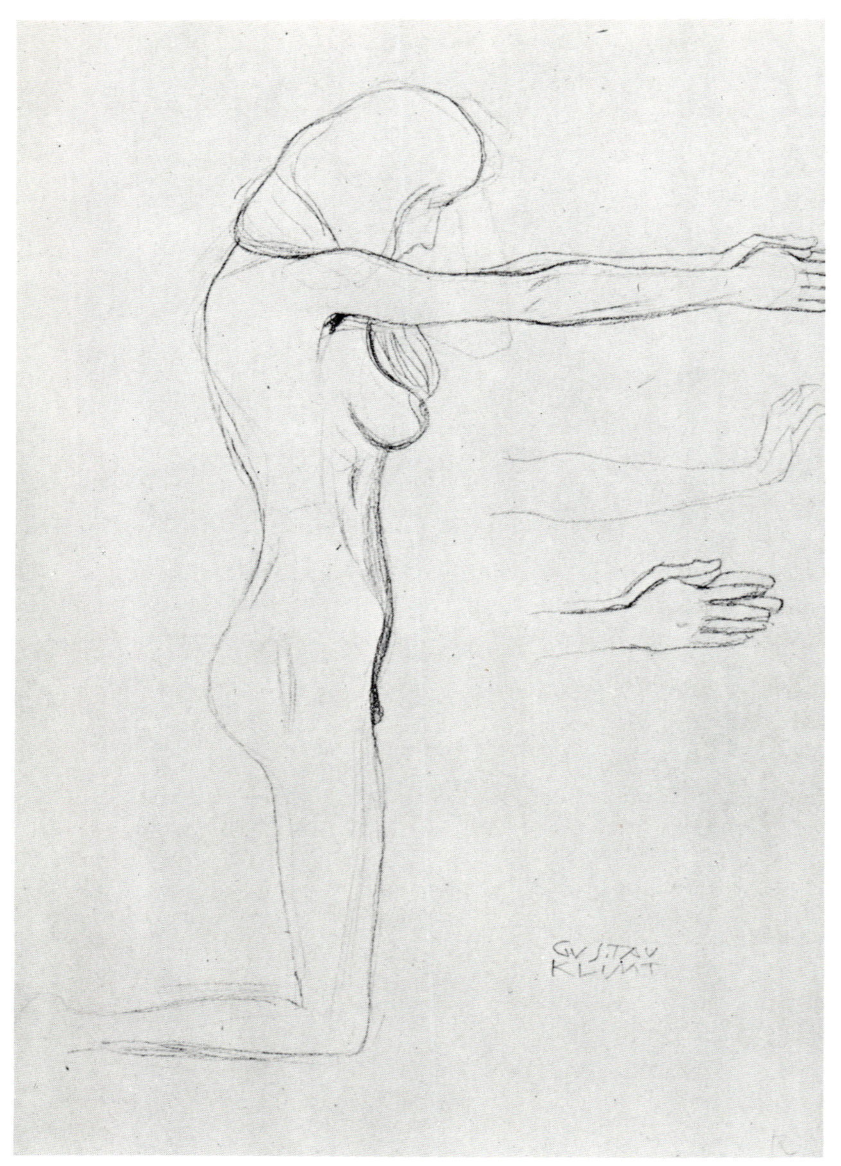

◁ *Gustav Klimt*
Study for the kneeling woman in the Sufferings of Weak Humanity. Black chalk.

▷ *Gustav Klimt*
Reversed study for the standing girl in the Sufferings of Weak Humanity. Black chalk.

This heroic transfiguration of goddess into Gorgon was also completed under the aegis of Nietzsche. The emaciated Humanity who beseeches the knight and borrows from the Belgian sculptor George Minne (represented by plasters in the exhibition reading room) her sinuous lines whose fragile undulation clings to the skeleton (even more than is the case with the model whose image is preserved in one of the lovely preliminary studies) longs to be led by the hero to the "superhumanity" beyond the monstrous bestial "subhumanity" represented in the second panel. This was the vocabulary used as a matter of course by Joseph August Lux in his commentary in *Deutsche Kunst und Dekoration* in 1902. And Nietzsche may also be the source ("The sufferings of genius and their value" in *Human, All Too Human*) of the curious association

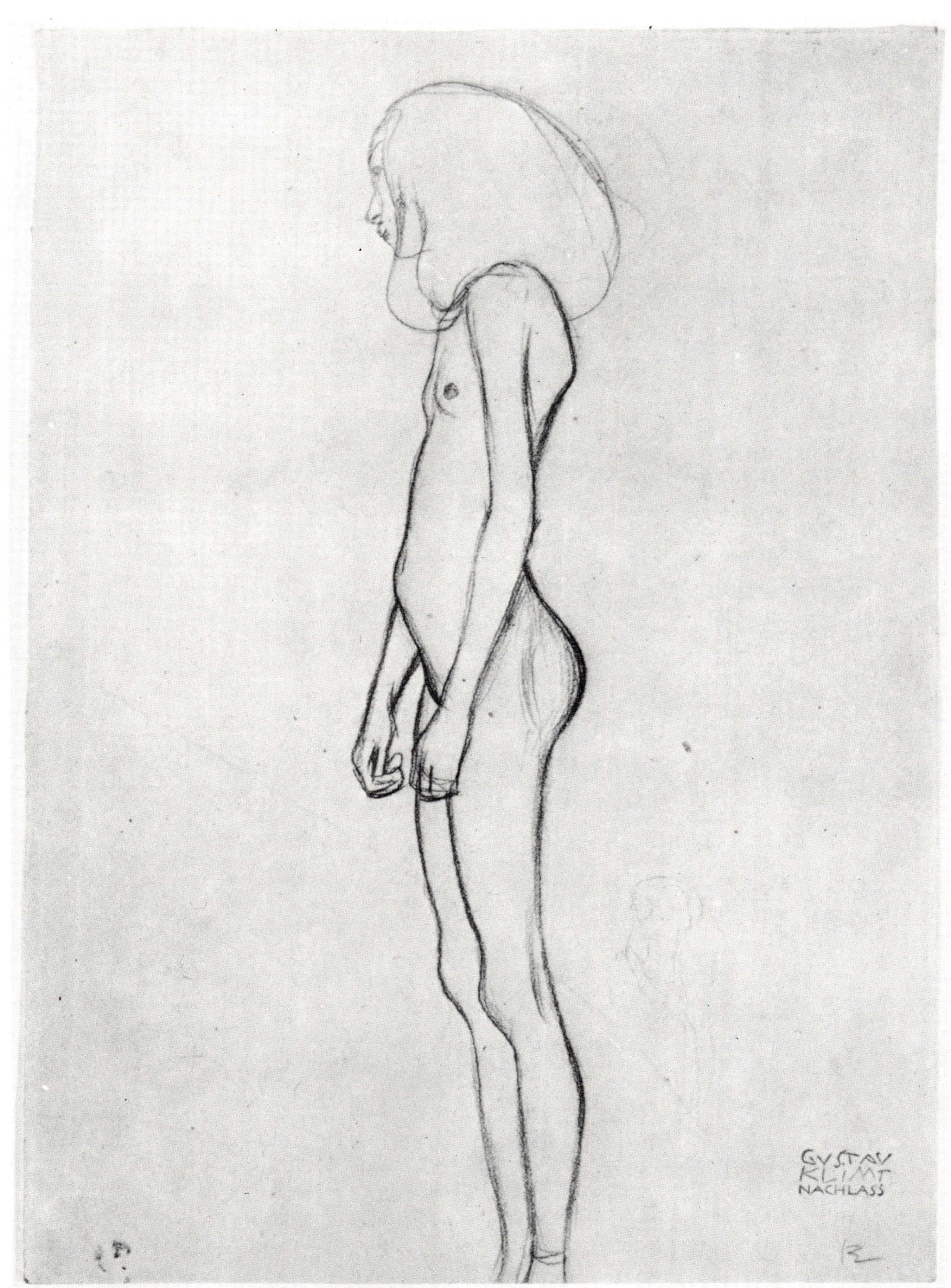
GUSTAV
KLIMT
NACHLASS

Left panel: The Sufferings of Weak Humanity.

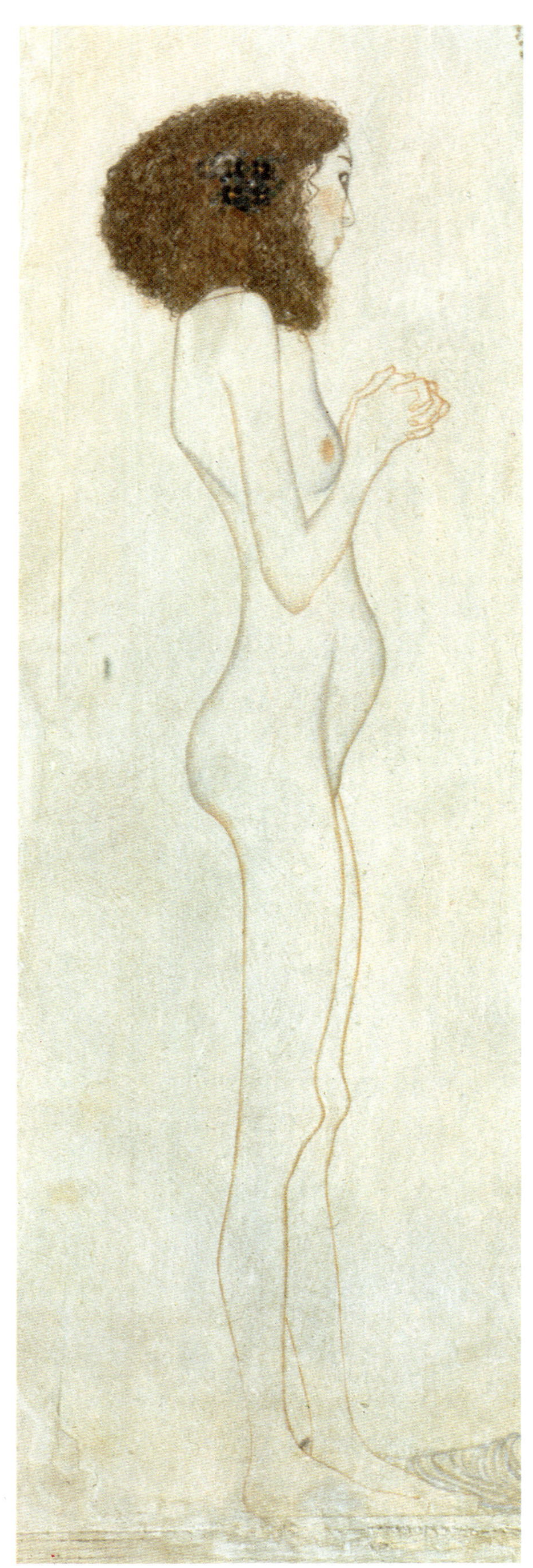

Left panel: The Sufferings of Weak Humanity.

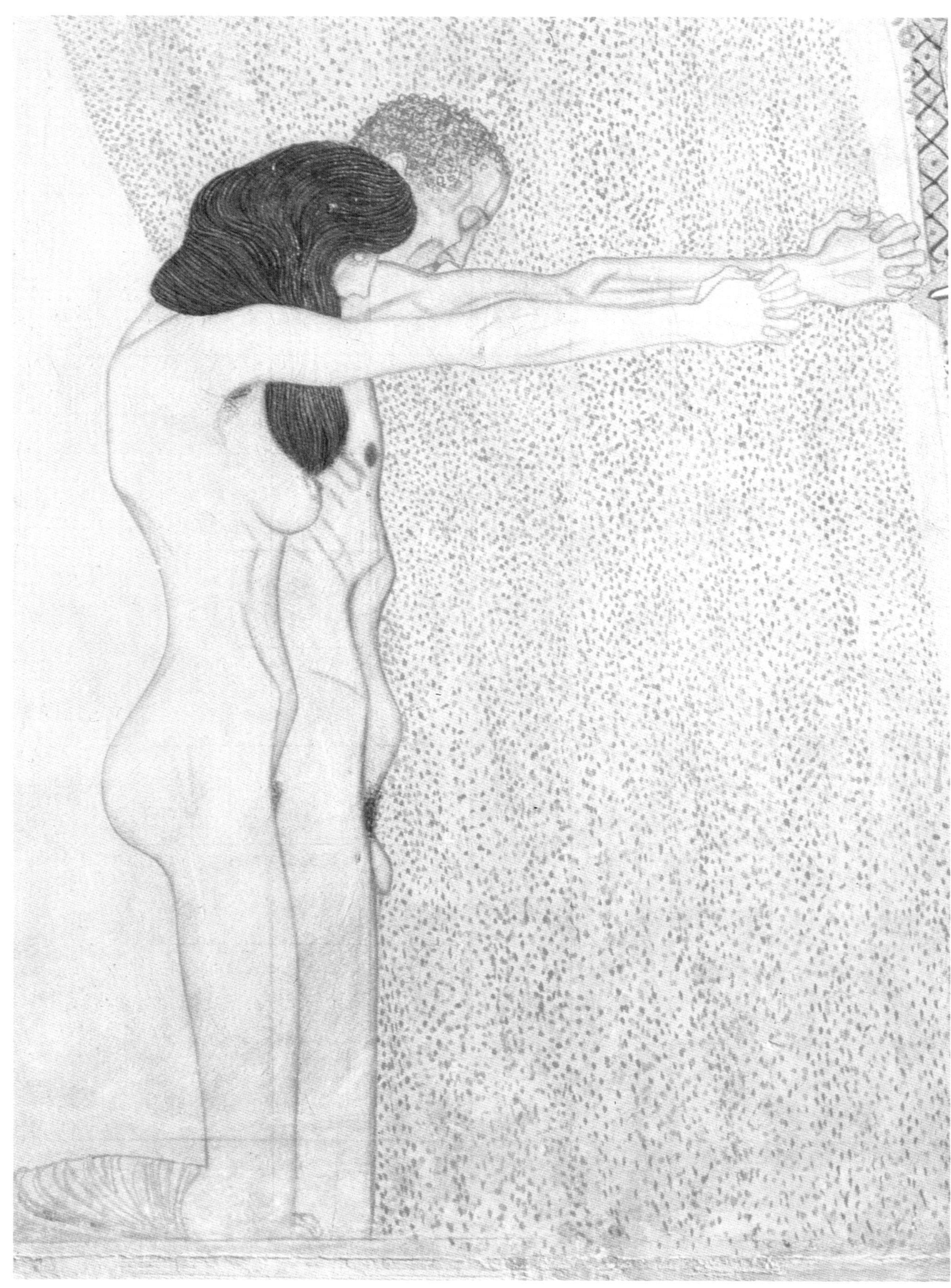

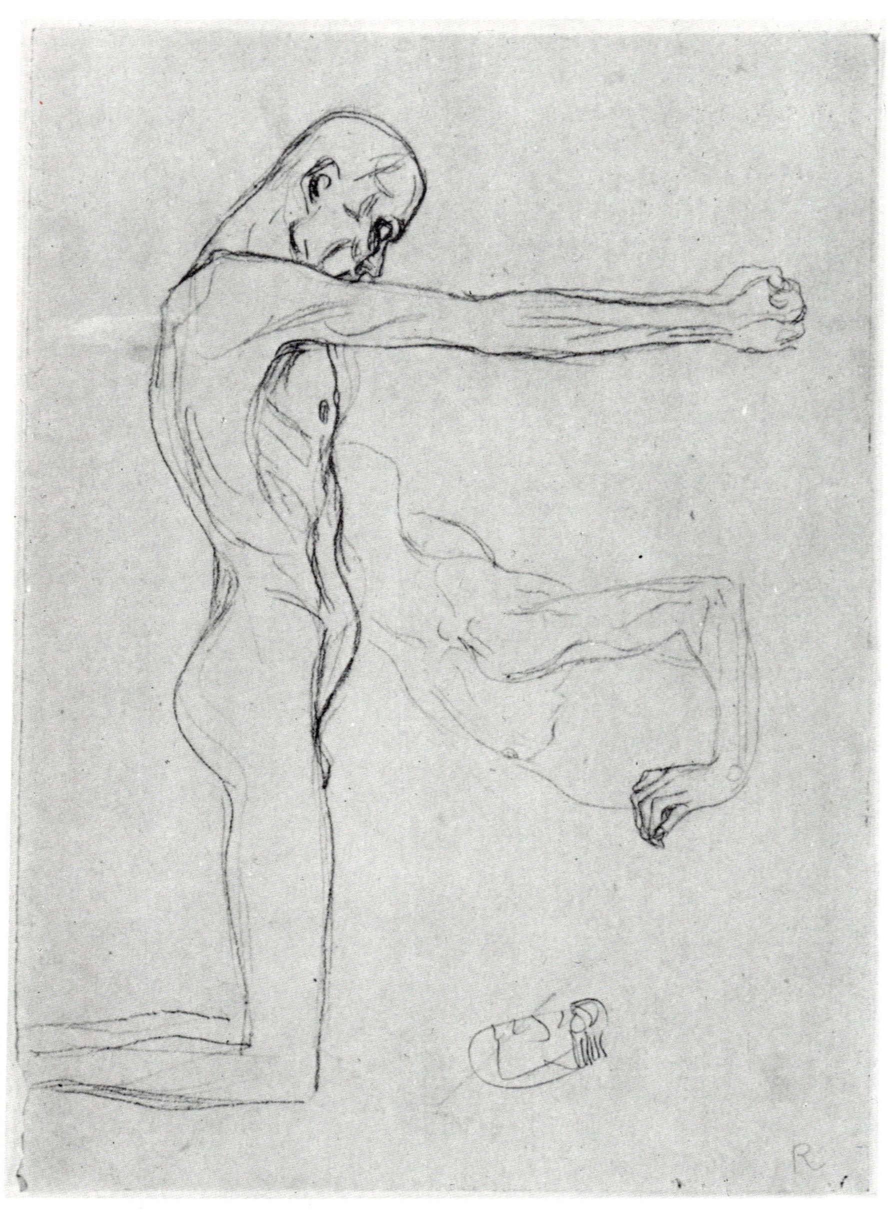

Gustav Klimt
Study for the kneeling man in the Sufferings of Weak Humanity. Black chalk.

of the knight with the internal driving powers, Pity, echoing the maiden's entreaty, and Ambition, with the squarish face typical of Khnopff, promising laurels. But obviously Klimt's most important task is to reach the golden silhouette of the warrior, engraved in profile in the stucco mosaic and fixed to the wall by upholstery tacks. In the following year he was to provide an astonishing and admirable counterpart: the recently rediscovered *Golden Knight*, the first title of which, *Life is a Battle* (*Das Leben ein Kampf*), clearly indicates the intended meaning of the two works. In 1904, a year before the final rejection of the University panels, *Goldfish* and *The Golden Knight* were exhibited simultaneously in Dresden. Klimt had replied to the public; the hero continued his struggle.

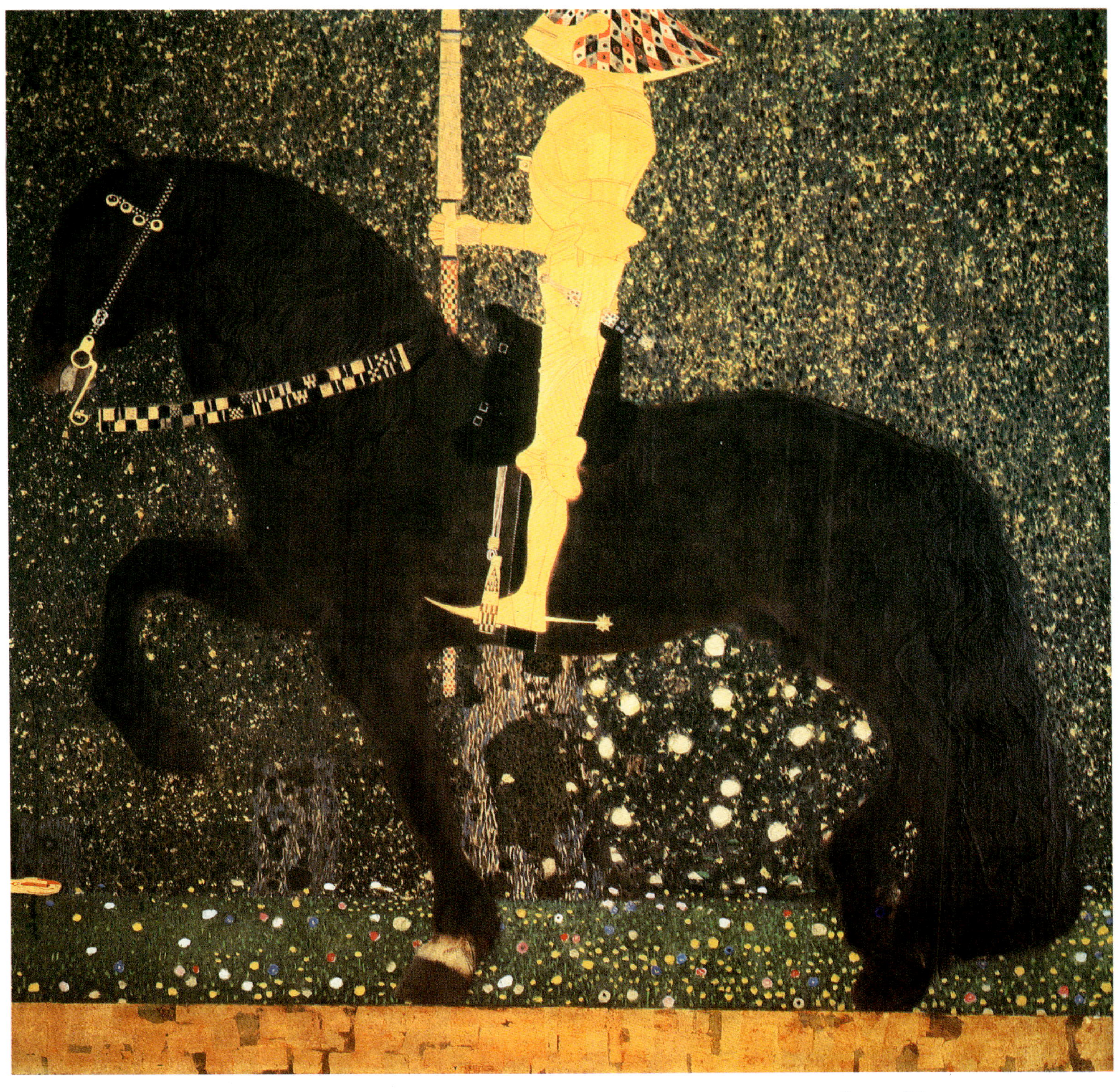

Gustav Klimt
Life is a Battle
(The Golden Knight), 1903. Oil.

In the next panel the first Hostile Powers thus give an amplified version of the redoubtable Medusa: no longer the decapitated head on the shield of Athene, or the three propitiatory heads of the Furies nailed above the entrance to the Secession Building, as at the Areopagus, but the forces of evil in the flesh, their long hair entwined with serpents, which were also to hold pride of place in the centre of *Jurisprudence*. The only diagonal figure in the frieze, because of

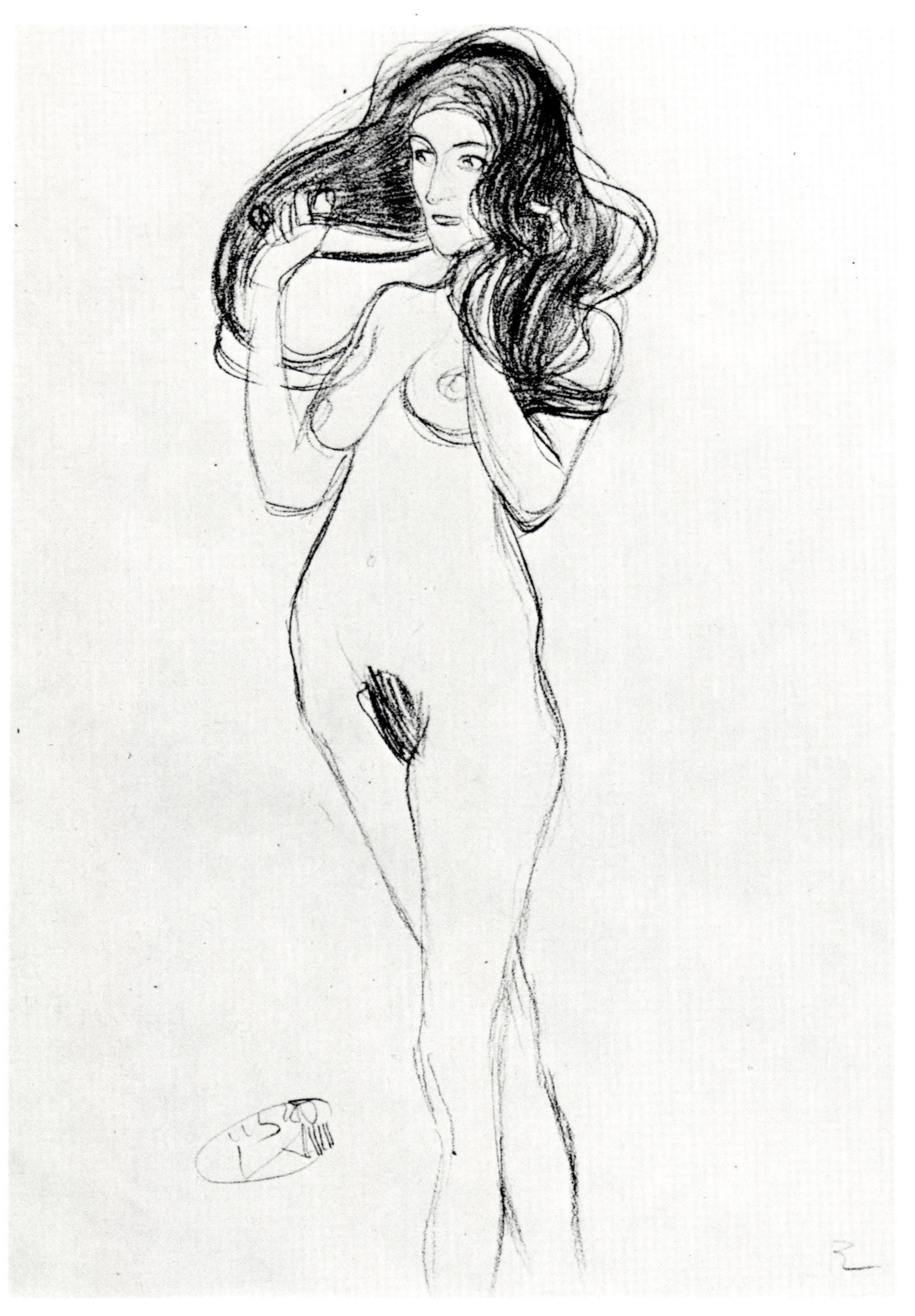

Gustav Klimt
Study for the Gorgons. Black chalk.

Central panel: Group of the three Gorgons and the figures above them, Sickness, Madness and Death.

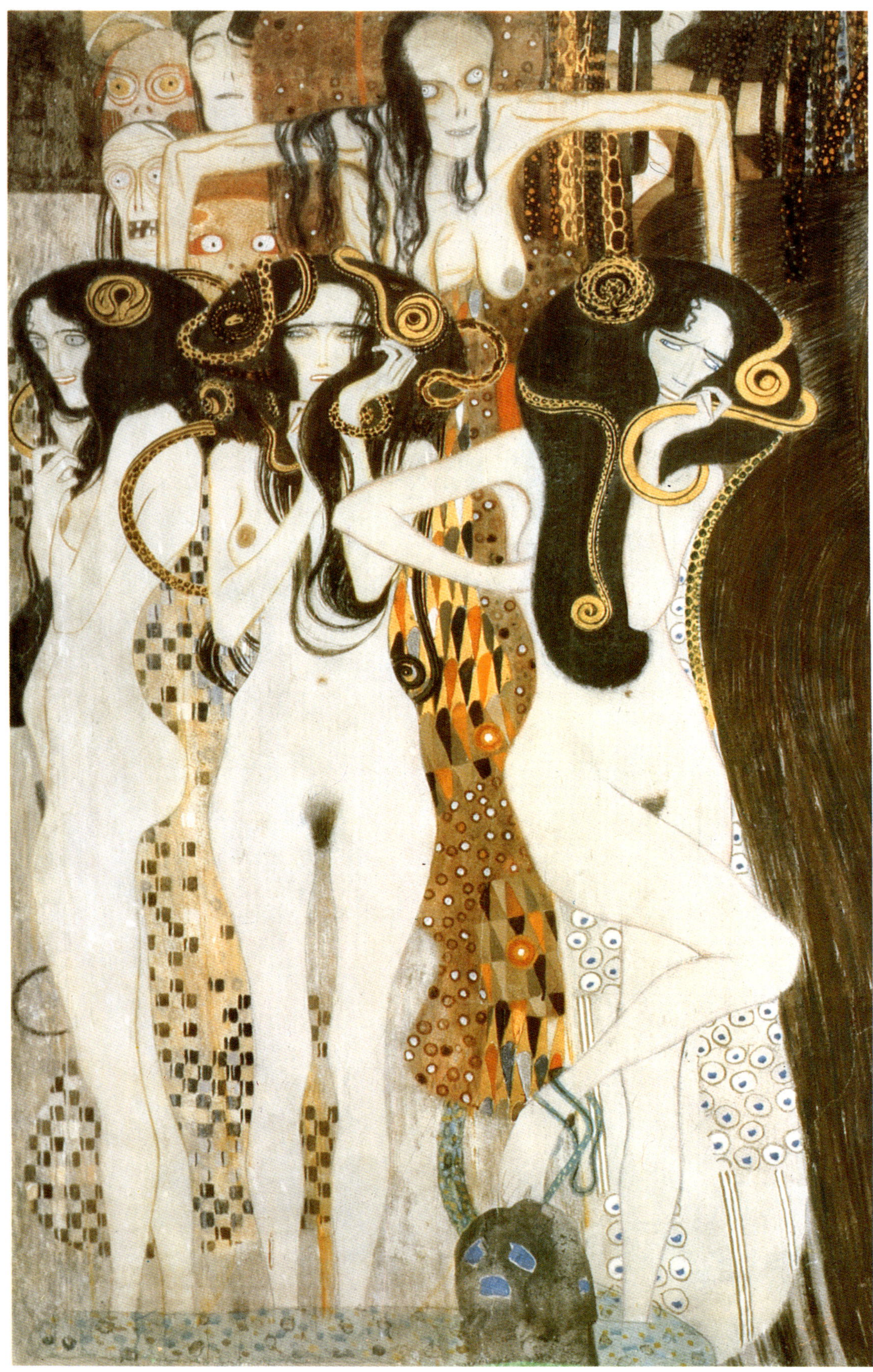

the position of her right leg and arm, which appears even in the first preliminary study, the last Gorgon undulates and bends forward to seal a closer alliance with Typhon, the ape with mother-of-pearl eyes who, unlike the Minotaur, looks far from being defeated. Klimt emphasizes in his catalogue notes that he was the only monster who momentarily triumphed over the Gods, in this case the Zeus-Beethoven by Klinger-Phidias enthroned in the neighbouring hall. As for the three scandalous figures of Lust, Lewdness and Excess (which borrows from Beardsley and Dürer's magnificent *Nemesis*), they may come from a line in the *Ode to Joy* ("Lust was given to the worm," *Wollust war dem Wurm gegeben*), as the neighbouring death's head, which Typhon holds under his paw and is echoed below by a medallion of Ernst Stöhr's, would seem to indicate. But they also correspond in their provocative exhibitionism to the *Goldfish* shown at the thirteenth exhibition, which Klimt wanted to dedicate to his critics. With *Nagging Care* in isolation (like the solitary figure pushed to the extreme left of Auchentaller's frieze, which merely transcribes Schiller's text literally: let the man who cannot find one kindred spirit "steal away in tears from this alliance"), the Beethovenesque struggle is amplified by a much more explicit attack on the maleficences of the contemporary world of which the Secession and Klimt in particular were victims.

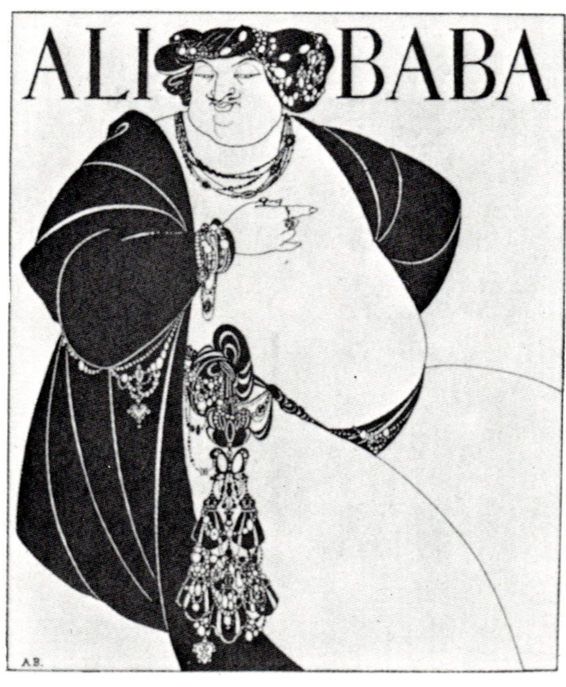

Aubrey Beardsley (1872-1898):
Cover for Ali Baba and the Forty Thieves, *1897.*

Central panel: Group of Lewdness, Lust and Excess.

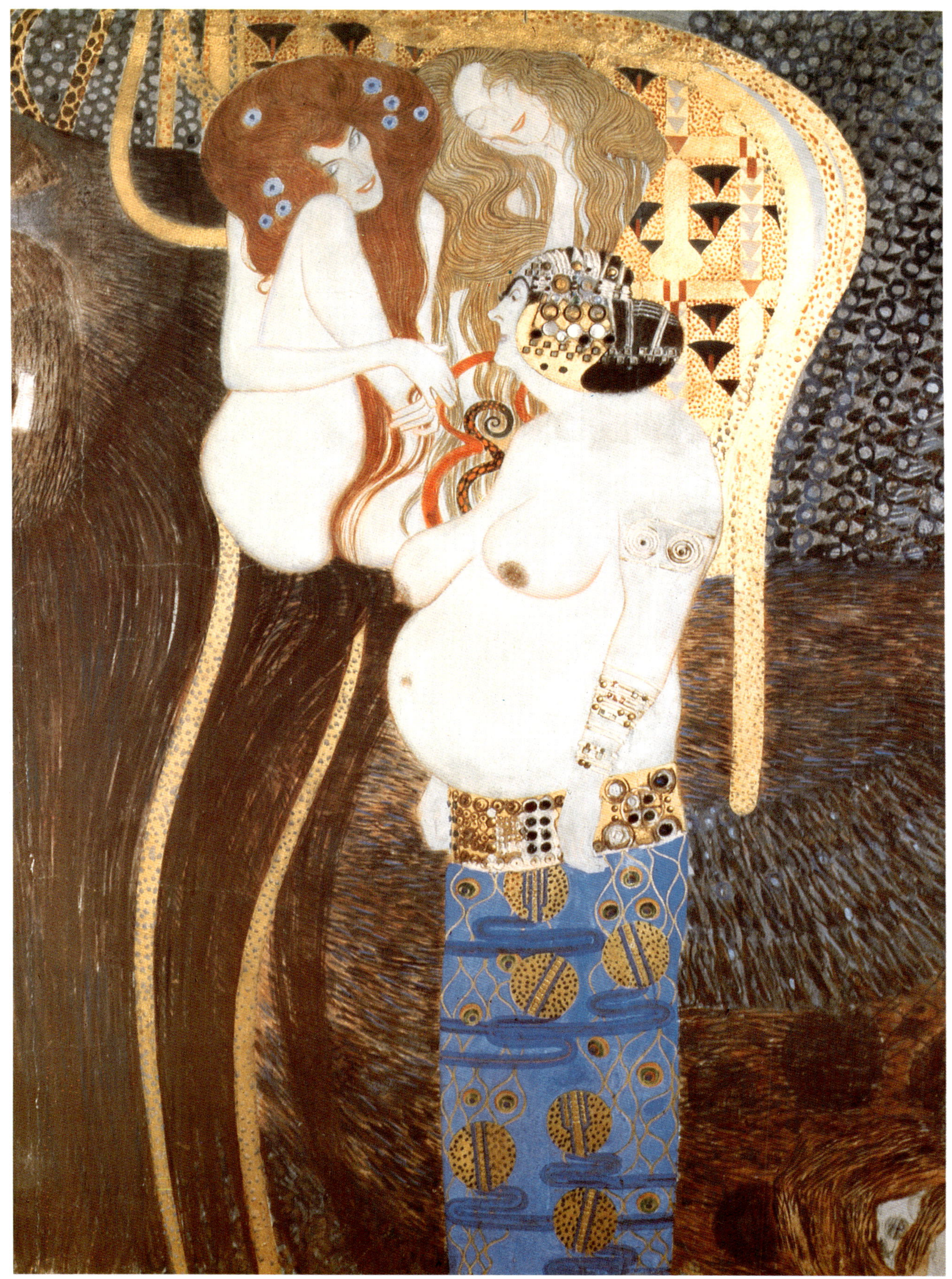

Central panel: The Giant Typhon.

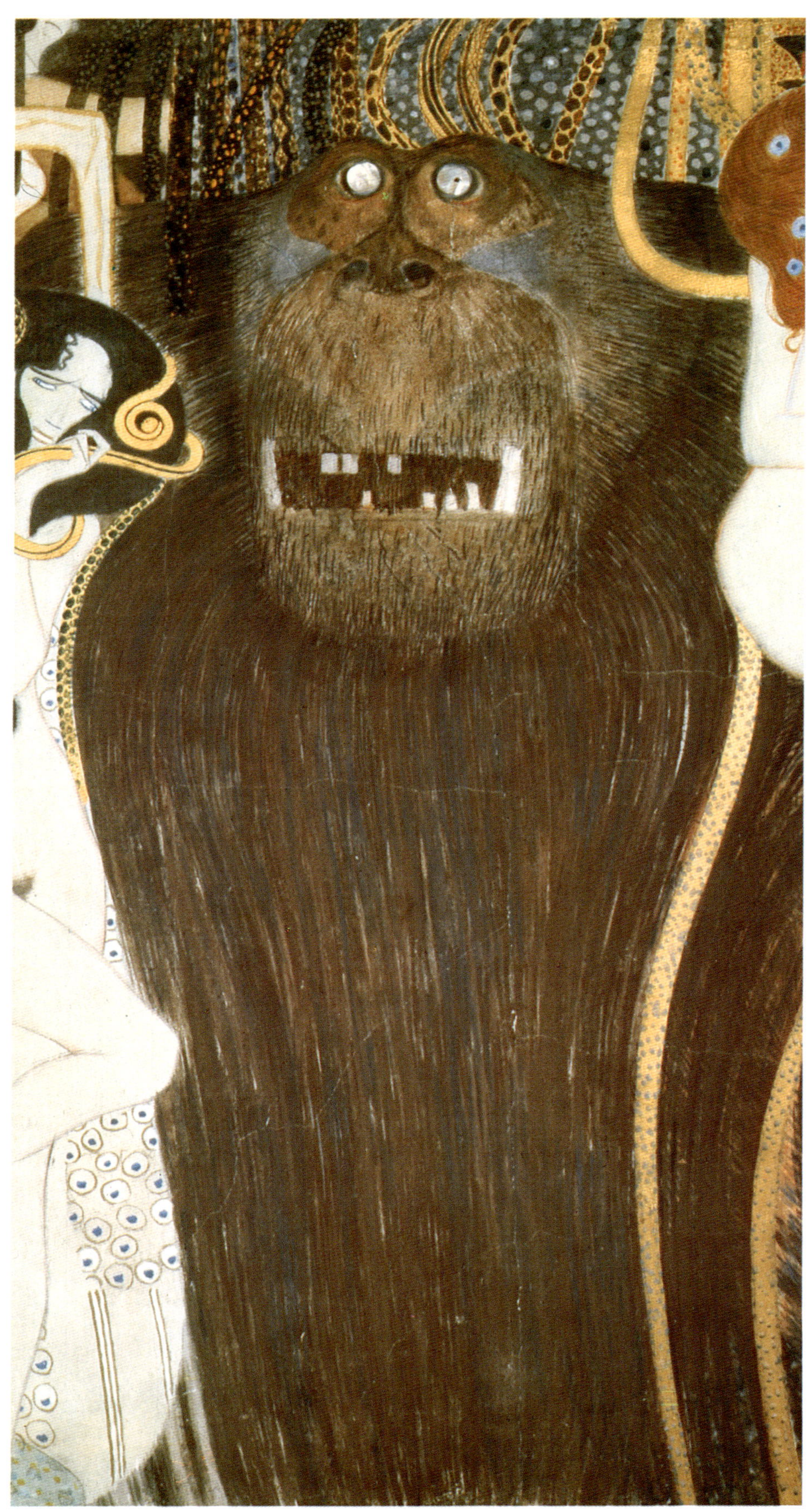

Central panel: Nagging Care.

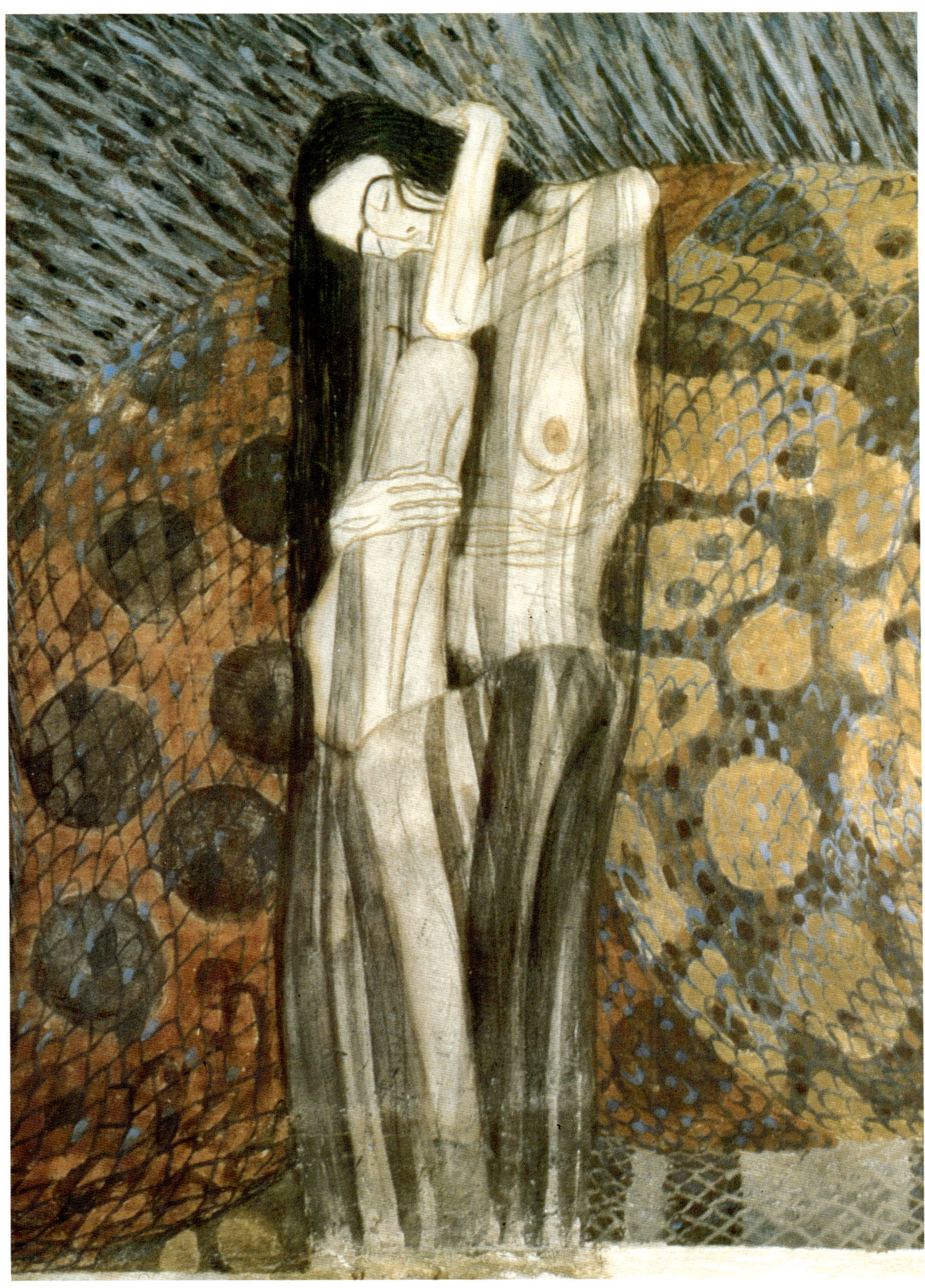

Right panel: Poetry.

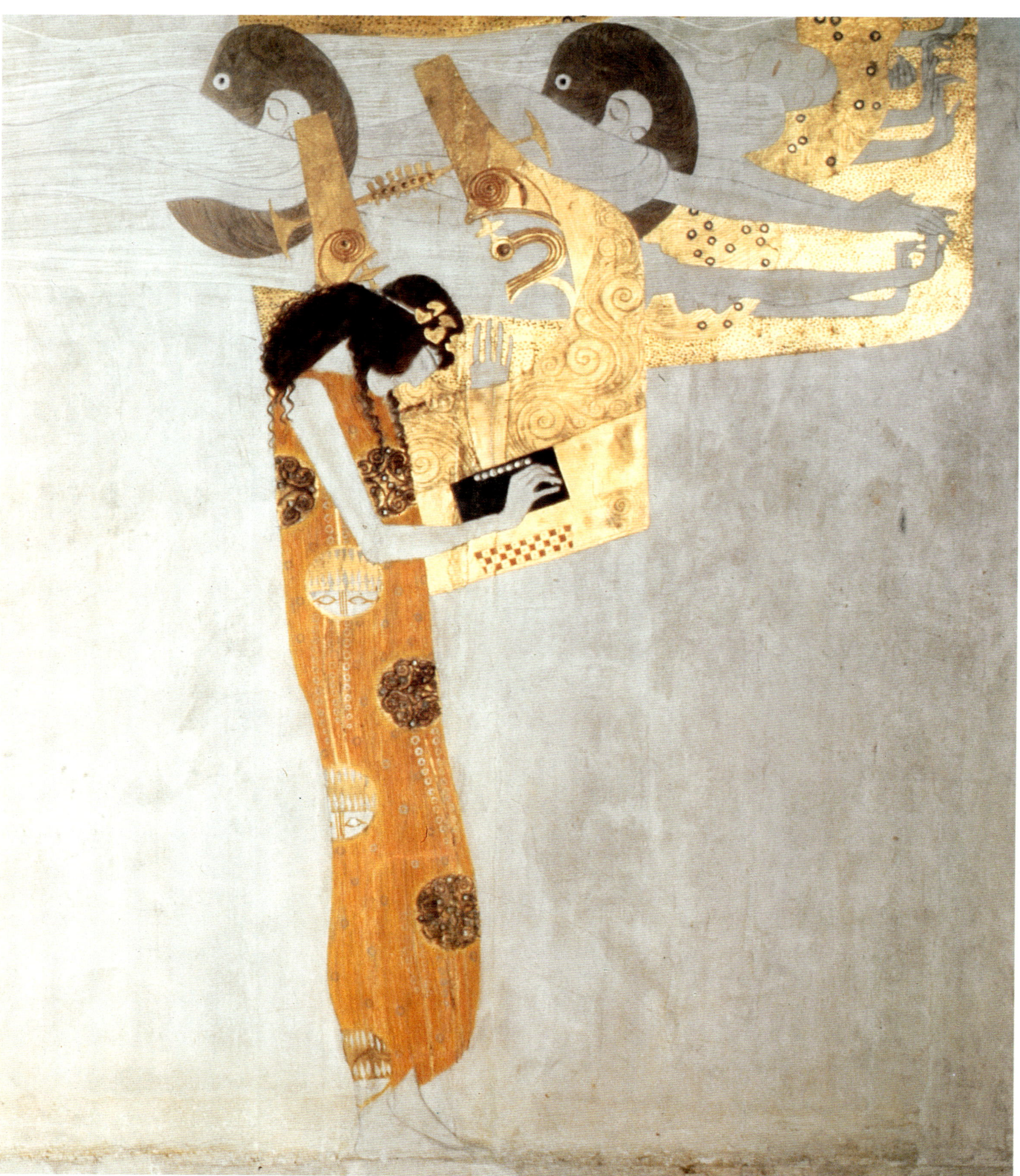

Right panel: The Choir of Heavenly Angels.

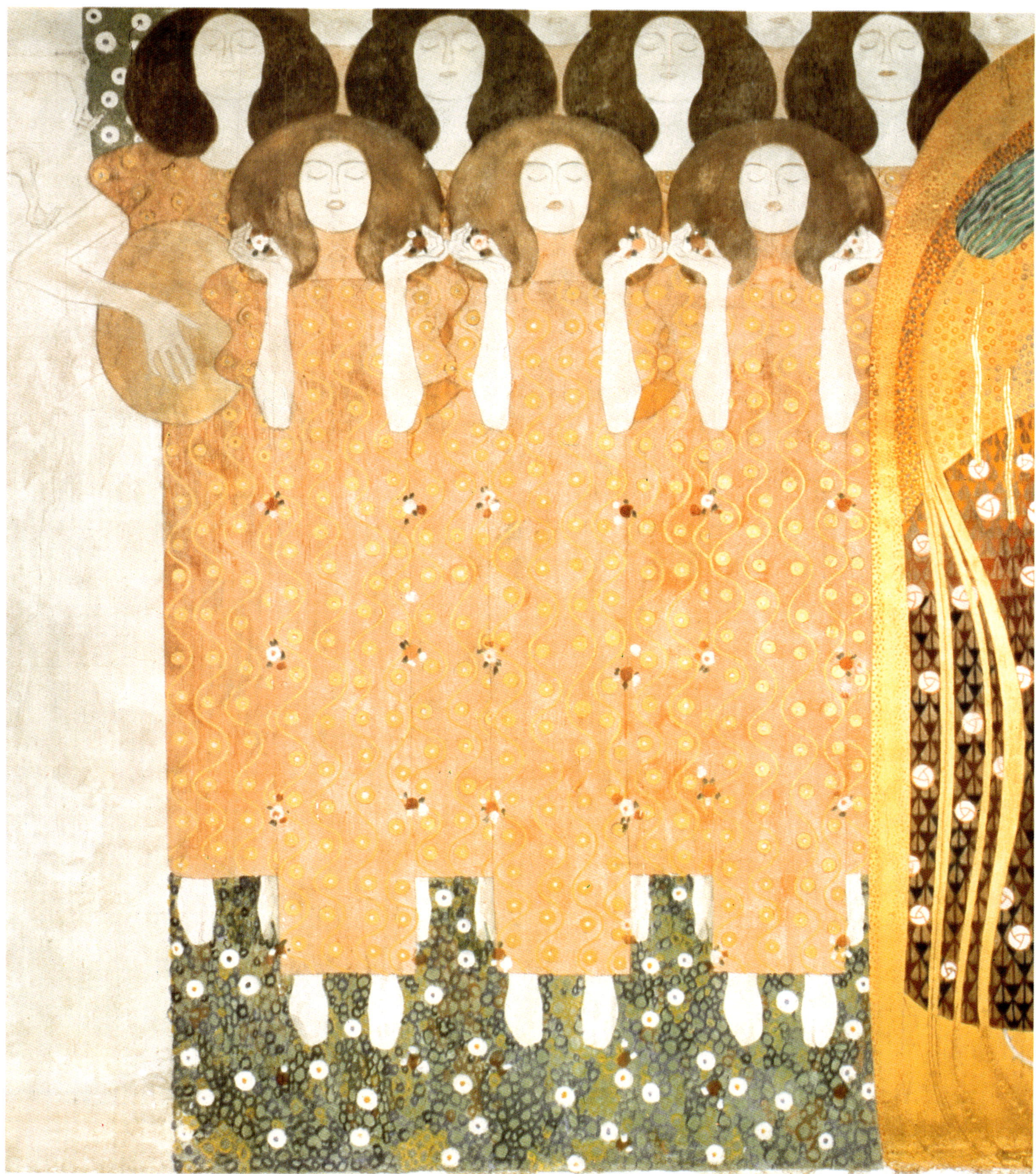

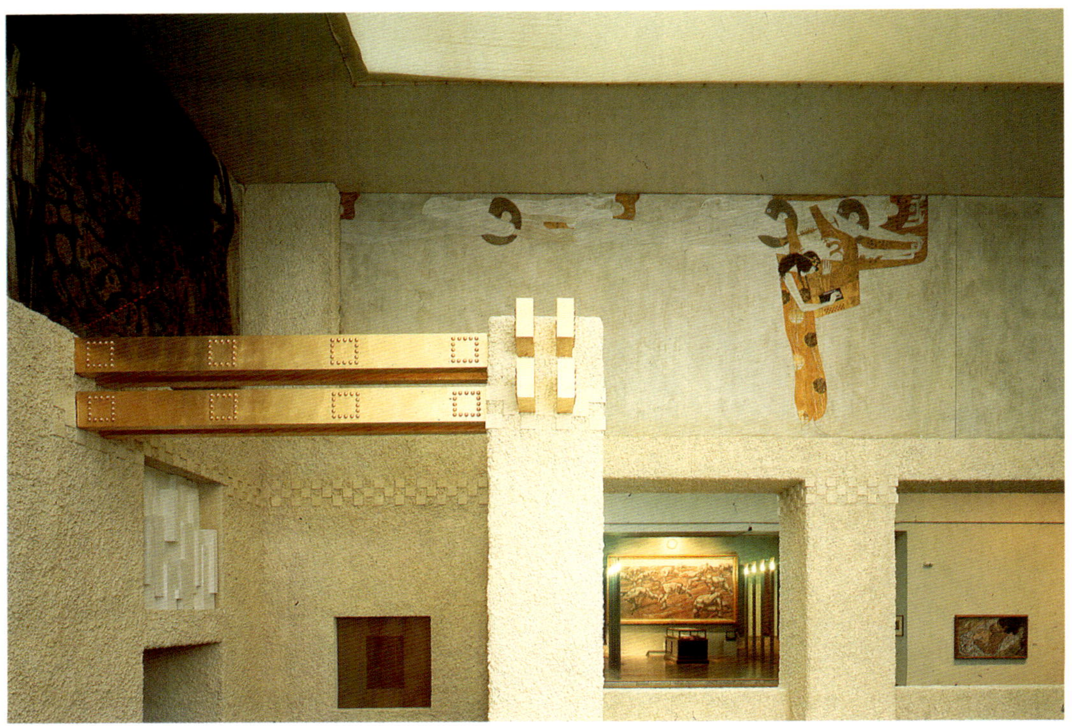

Reconstructions of the Klimt Room by the architectural workshop of Professor Hans Hollein, 1985.

On the next wall, Poetry, with her lyre and her distinctly antiquizing forms, offers a "repose" which suggests too obviously the expected victory of Athene. The true reply is further on after the entry of the choir (female, unlike Beethoven's at this point) which borrows from Hodler its parallel disincarnate figures hovering above the fields of Paradise. The hero then finds genuine fulfilment in a kiss, which is no longer fraternal and liberating, but egoistic and anti-world, in the midst of a *hortus conclusus* whose stylization this time comes straight from Mackintosh (the rose-tree, and its flattened three-petalled flowers, as well as the protective "bell" sheltering the couple, which already figured in the main panel exhibited by the Scottish artist in 1900). The comets' tails, the emblems of the sun and the moon, correspond to the cosmogony of the main hall, to the Day and Night of Böhm and Roller, but are merely passive witnesses. And this final kiss, placed facing inwards above the entrance at the end of the frieze visit, seems to conclude to its own advantage and at the expense of the Klinger which is only glimpsed and to which it is no longer really necessary to pay homage. Klimt has finally substituted his own response for the struggle of Beethoven (and later Wagner), a response comparable in its way to Mahler's when, in the penultimate movement of his Third Symphony (finished in 1896), he sets to music not Schiller, but Nietzsche and the "Drunken Song" of Zarathustra which evokes "Joy, deeper than the heart's agony" and wants "deep, deep, deep eternity"—a vision of the world markedly different from the Beethovenesque *Durch Leiden Freude* (Joy through Suffering).

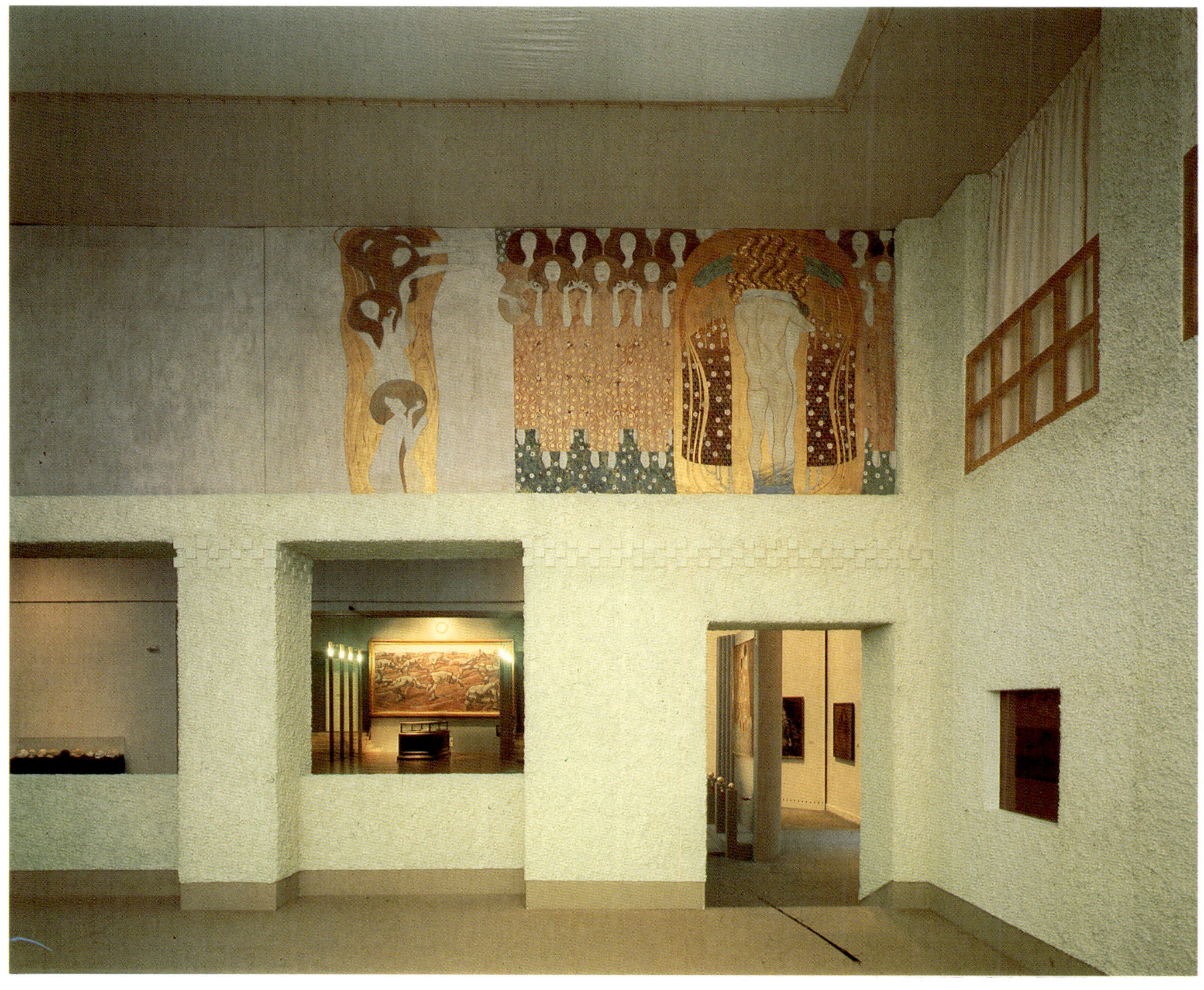

V
Themes

By asking us not to go too deeply into the very generalized allegory of the Longing for Happiness, Ludwig Hevesi, the best Viennese critic of the day and the most favourable to Klimt, has led subsequent critics badly astray. His refusal to take the precise meaning of the images and their resonances into account stems from the identical attitude adopted by contemporary Vienna, which also turned away from the world in order to formalize it.

Nevertheless Klimt's *personal themes* are imprinted even more emphatically on the already dense *iconographical* tissue which

Ferdinand Hodler (1853-1918):
The Chosen One, 1893-1894. Tempera and oil.

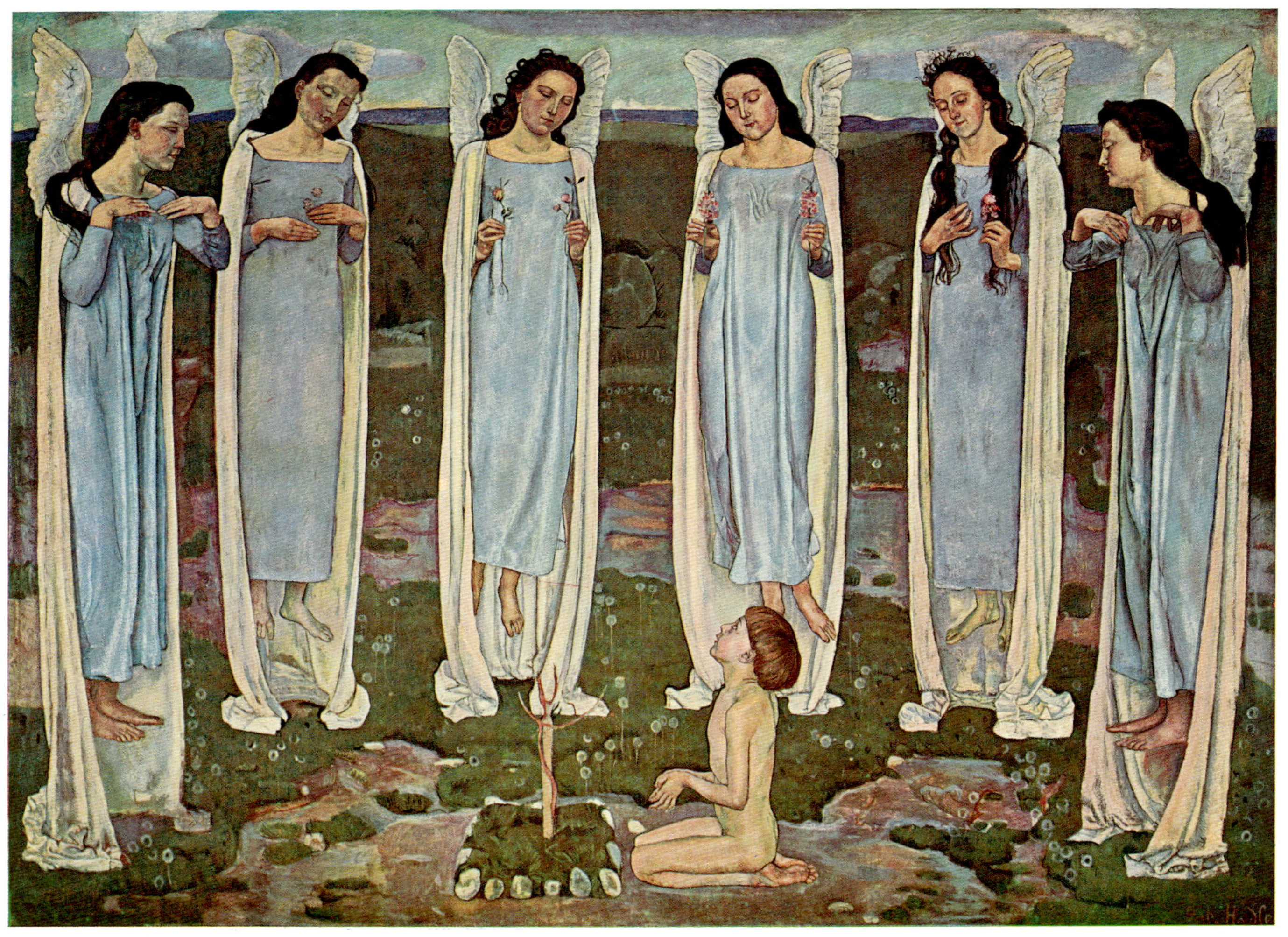

Right panel: This Kiss for the Whole World.

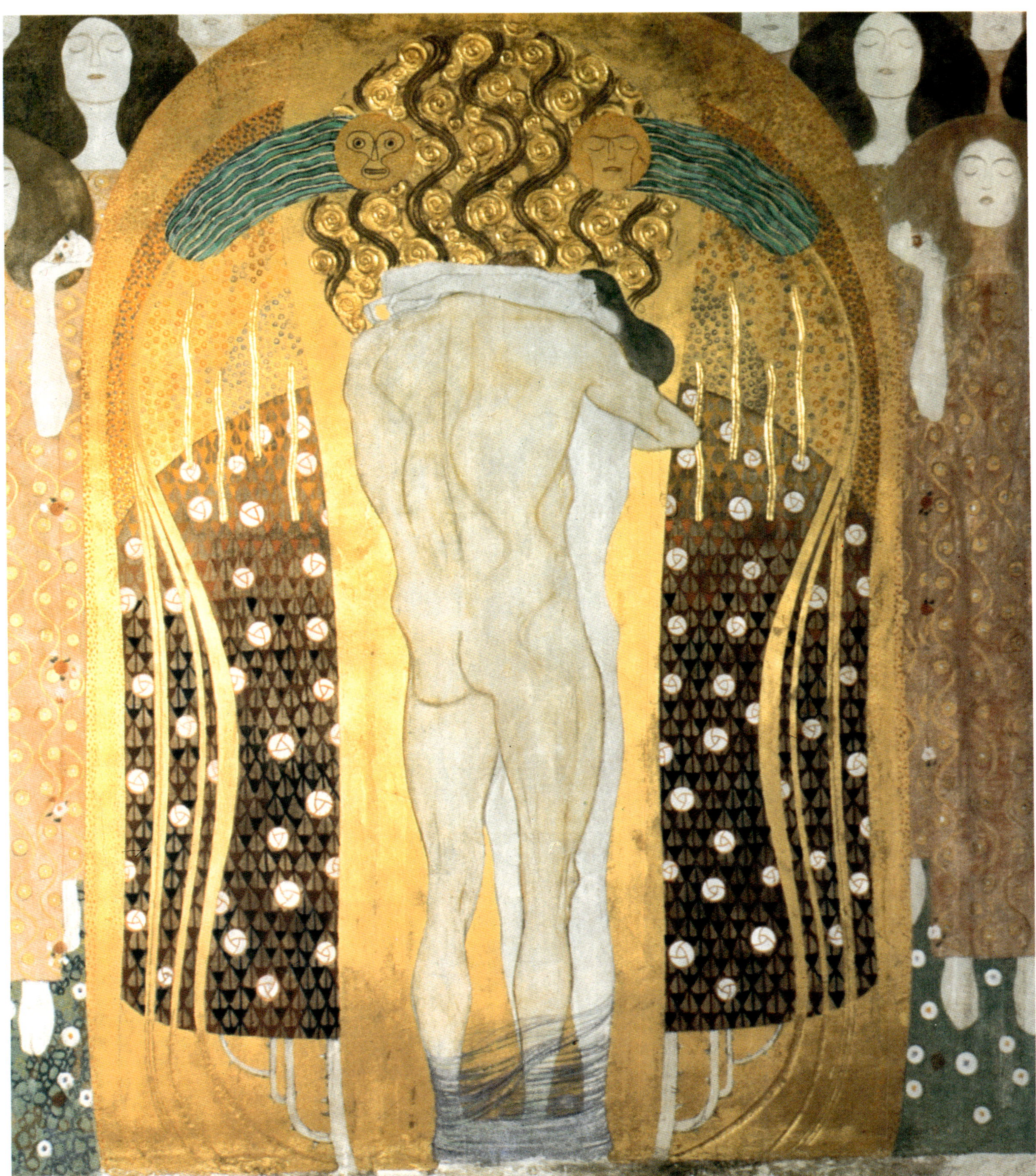

simply reinforces the compulsory direction for viewing the frieze by enriching it. The result is that in many respects they cancel out its movement and run counter to the effects that were consciously sought. It is this "overloading" which ultimately differentiates Klimt's frieze from the other participants' works.

In actual fact, everything starts from the central panel, a dark patch between the other two with a compact ornate surface. More surely than the austere floating figures, it immediately catches the spectator in the trap of its female forms and their equally provocative looks. Here undisguised sexuality is affirmed as the frieze's real motive force.

It is from this angle that we should revert to the question of music, undoubtedly the work's mainstay, but perhaps not at the

Gustav Klimt
Music I, 1895. Oil.

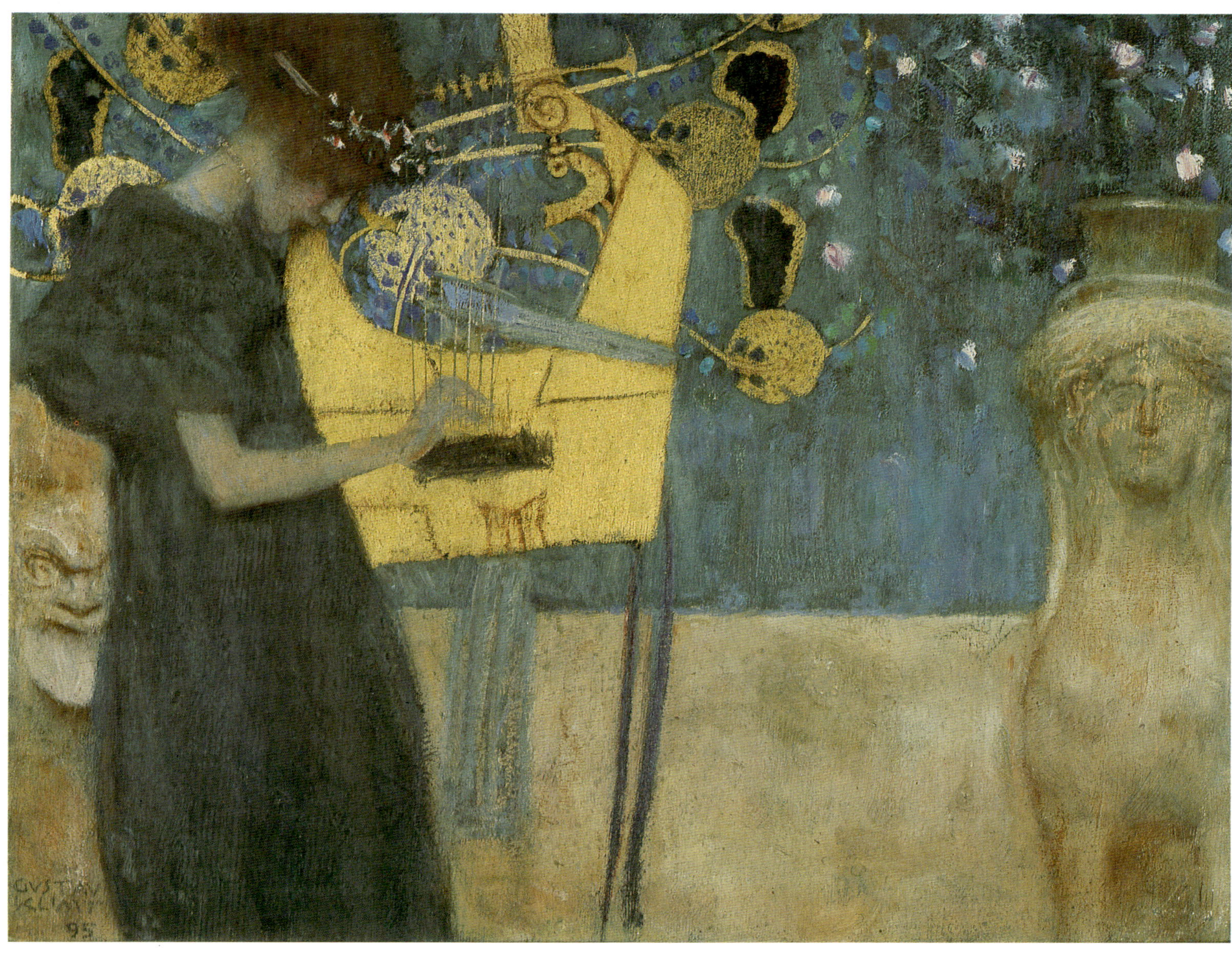

Right panel: Poetry.

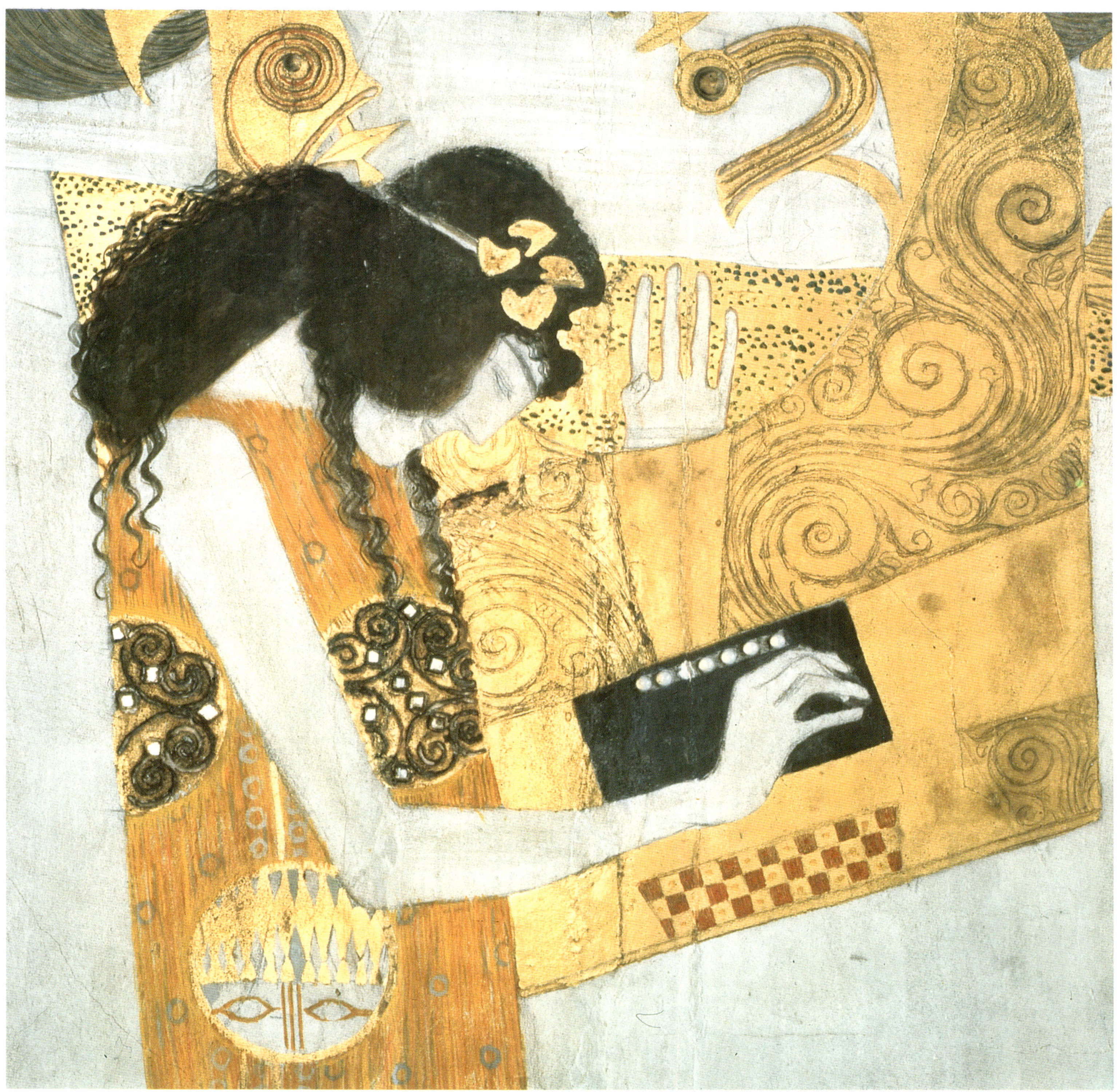

level one has seen. Klimt's earlier works dealing with the same subject, which are naturally involved in it, posed different problems, as Carl E. Schorske has pointed out. In 1895 *Music I* provides the perfect classical model for the woman who, with her delicate profile,

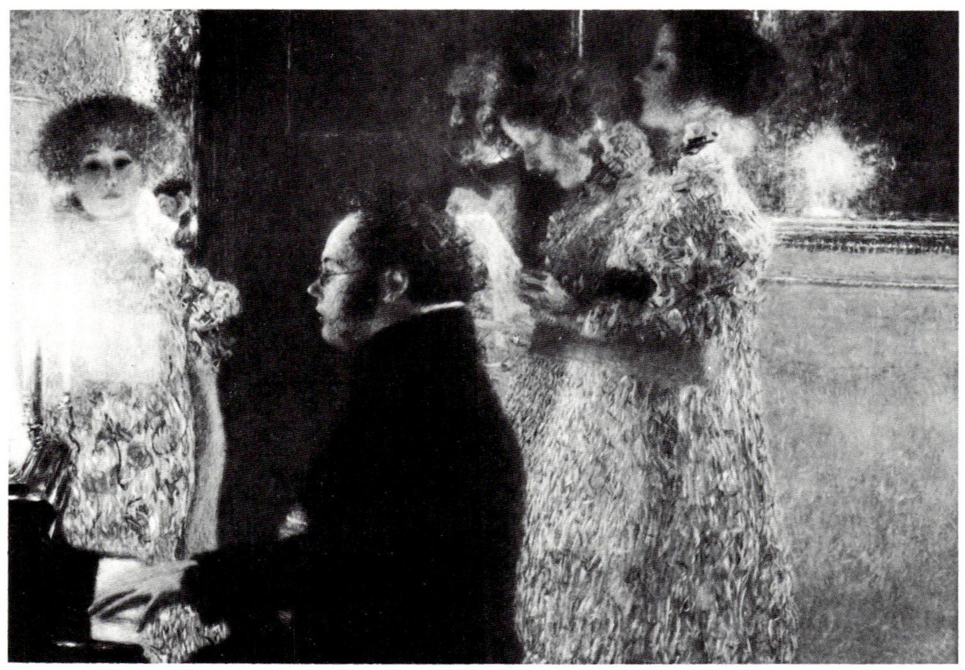

rapt expression and refound serenity under the sign of Athene (or Apollo), became the lyre player personifying Poetry in the Beethoven Frieze of 1902. But by associating her with a Sphinx and a mask of Silenus seen *front face*, the picture also mirrors the Nietzschean theories of the *Birth of Tragedy*. Alongside the measured song of Apollo implicit in the plastic perfection of the instrument, the Dionysiac forces of instinct, represented by a (female) body and the fascinating faces, also mount guard. In 1898 and 1899 the picture was duplicated in the two facing panels in the music room of

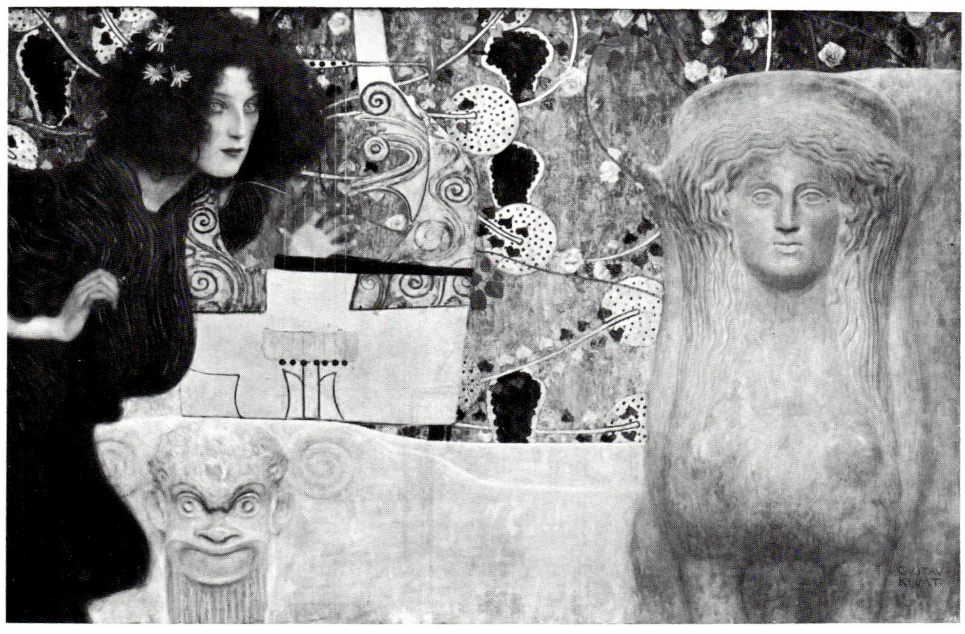

◁ *Gustav Klimt*
Schubert at the Piano, 1899 (destroyed in 1945). Oil.

▽◁ *Gustav Klimt*
Music II, 1898
(destroyed in 1945). Oil.

the Villa Dumba in Vienna (destroyed in 1945). *Schubert at the Piano* in *profile* reproduces the Apollonian serenity of the lyre player in an idealized Biedermeyer interior, whereas *Music II* makes a major change and replaces him with a typically Viennese female figure, with long hair and provocative curves, who, placed parallel to the Sphinx, now *looks out* at the spectator. In 1902 *both* versions of *Music*, not only its ethereal sublimating version, are shown in the frieze. By way of a vignette published in *Ver Sacrum* in 1901, *Music I* has become Poetry—also a characteristic change of name! As for the Dionysiac *Music II*, it no longer needs instruments. The female figures of the central panel suffice to capture its image. The struggle is *also* there and it is not Poetry alone (repression of impulses and sublimation) that indicates its outcome, nor even the group of the Arts and a completely idealized choir of angels, but the final couple glorifying a love based wholly on sexuality.

Thus the frieze is lit by different light. The central panel is no longer that dark and rarely visited tunnel through which one has to pass quickly and fearfully to rejoin the flight of the floating figures. Sumptuously painted with care and love, it gives the key to the work: the interrogation of the Mystery, more specifically of feminine sexuality, conceived of as centre and origin of the world. And the final embrace *attempts* to supply *one* answer to the drama being played, around the Ninth Symphony, in the confrontation of woman and hero.

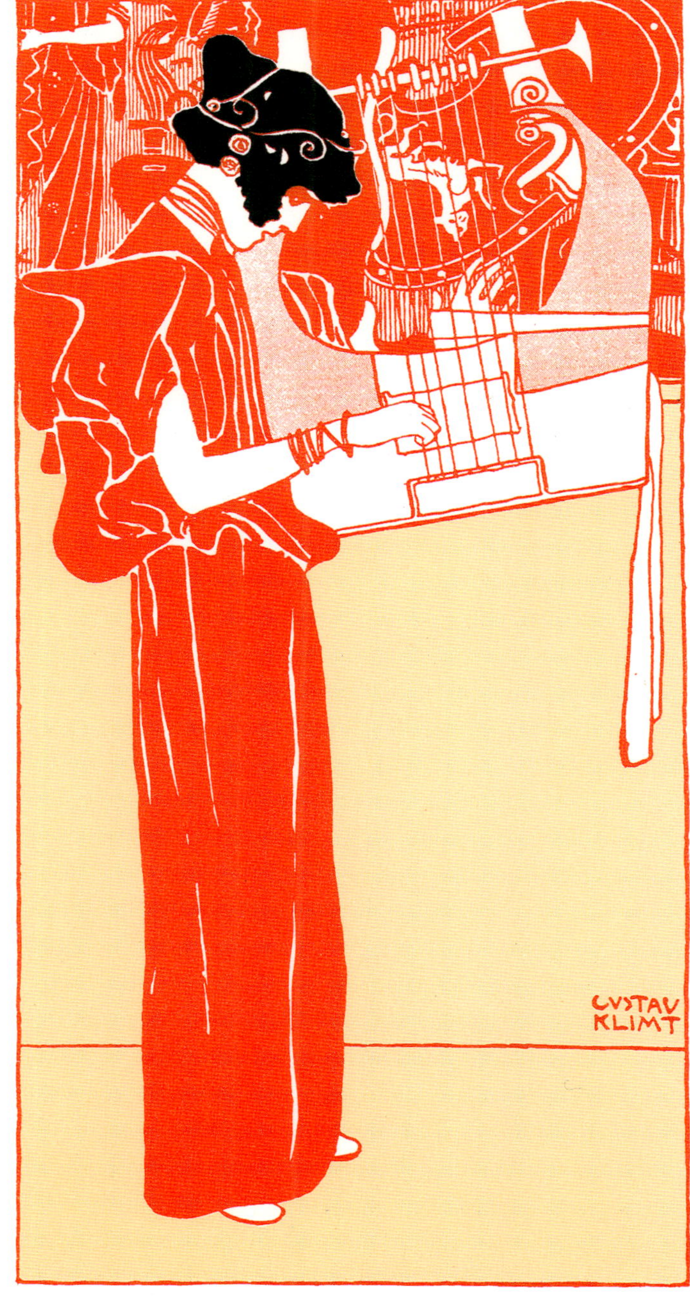

Gustav Klimt
Music, 1901.
Colour lithograph
published in Ver Sacrum, *Vienna, 1901.*

Central panel: Heads of Lewdness, Lust and Excess.

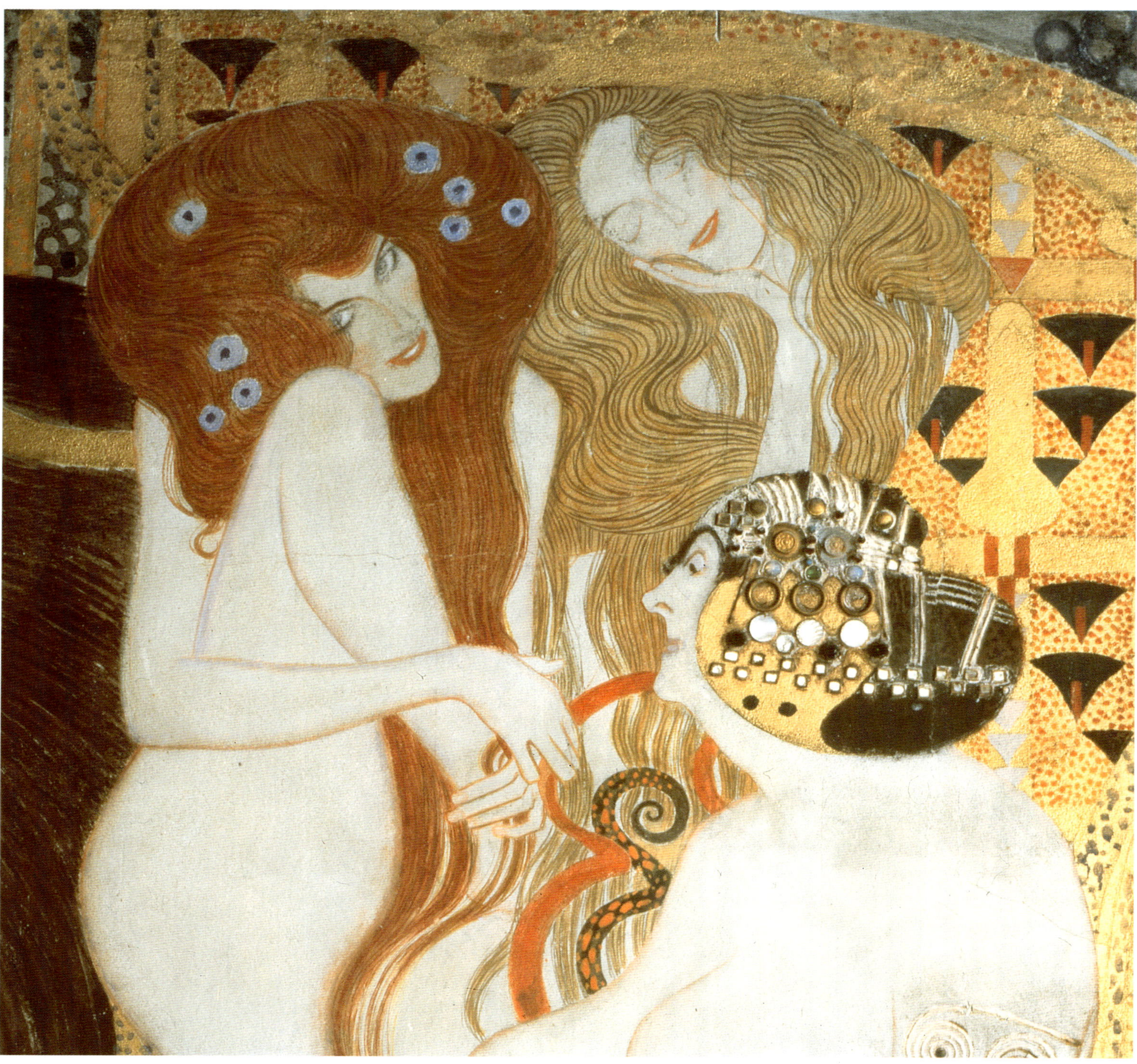

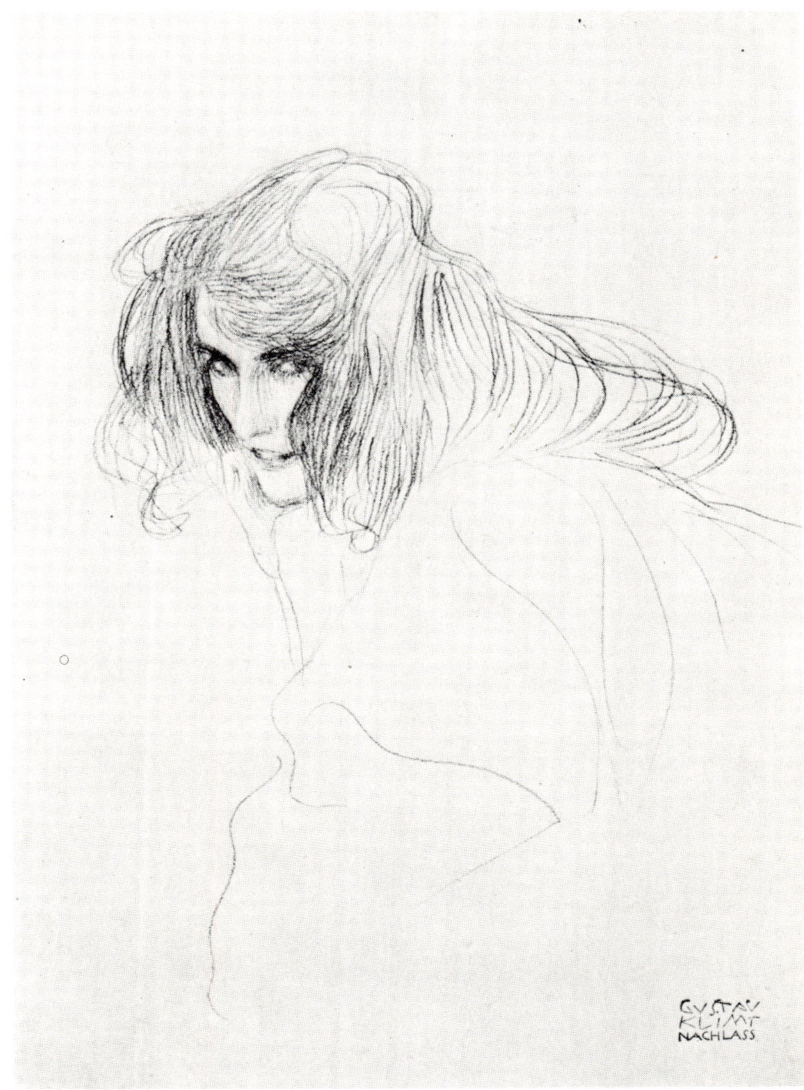

Gustav Klimt
Study related to Lewdness
(Portrait of Maria Janaich,
dancer at the Vienna Opera).
Black chalk.

Klimt himself could not be clearer in this respect when he places the group of the three scandal causers, Lust, Lewdness and Excess, certainly one of the high points of his work, in the *centre* of the frieze, surrounded by a phallus and a profusion of female sexual organs.

The fundamental voyeurism which lies at the base of his work, as Alessandra Comini has very justly remarked, is exhibited at the heart of the frieze with Lewdness (and not "lust": *Unkeuschheit*) on the left of the group (a figure modelled on a contemporary Viennese dancer). The frank ("lewd") revelation of her sexuality marks the end of the combination of eroticism and mysticism found in the international Symbolism of a Toorop or a Thorn Prikker (*The Bride*), as well as that exhibited by the androgynous protectresses who appear for the last time in 1901 together with Hygeia, in the foreground of *Medicine*. And it is in this revelation that Klimt can most fairly be compared with Freud.

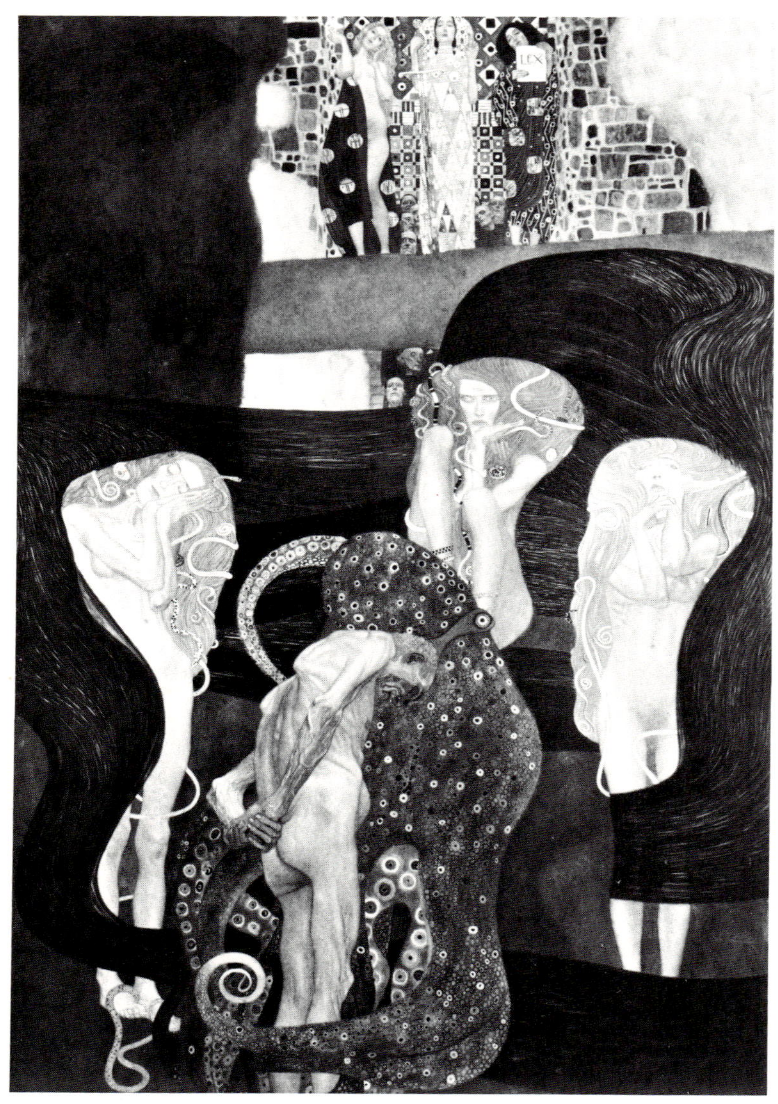

Gustav Klimt
Jurisprudence, 1903-1907
(destroyed in 1945). Oil.

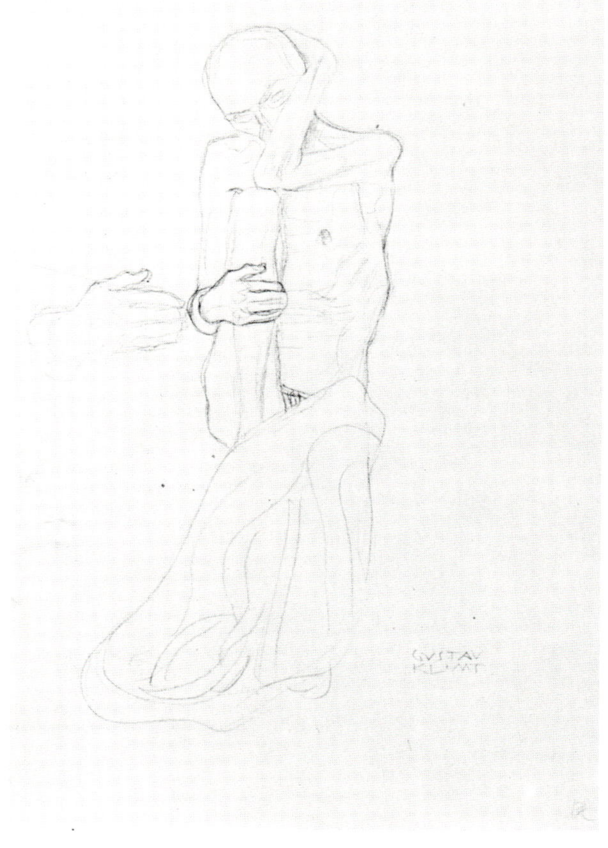

Gustav Klimt
Study for Nagging Care. Black chalk.

But the revelation, as with Freud, is still not a genuine liberation. On the contrary, it results in the dual nightmare of the female who castrates (by her actual sex this time and no longer by the indirect symbolism of *Judith I* of 1901) and of the "lustful" woman in whose case the pleasure suggested is primarily intended for herself (Lewdness and several erotic drawings by Klimt) and so constitutes a threat to man. The first type appears in the central panel in the form of the three Gorgons shown frontally and in profile, but in *Jurisprudence* the same three figures, this time associated with their victim, clearly show what they have in store for the guilty voyeur. The second appears in the symmetrical group on the other side of Typhon, but a little further on is complemented by *Nagging*

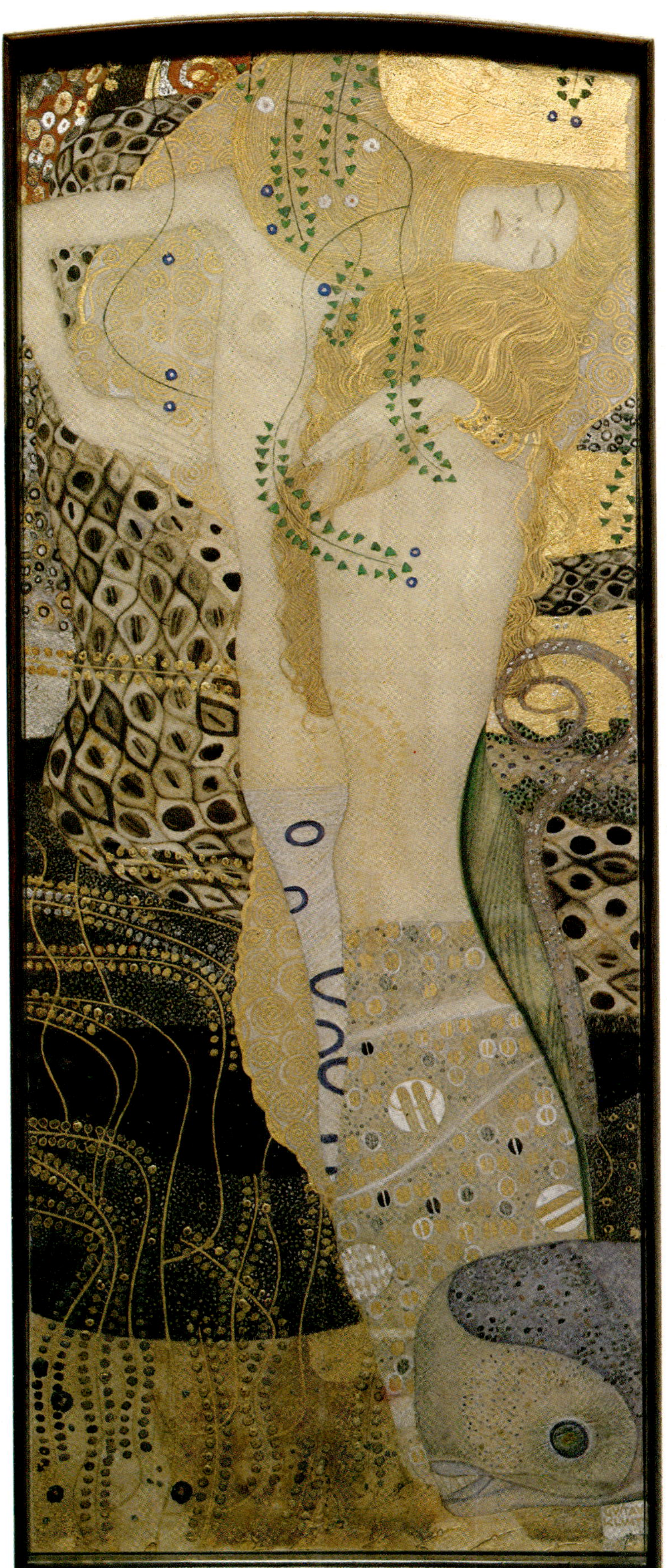

Gustav Klimt
Water Snakes I, 1904-1907. Mixed media.

Care, a fairly obvious contemporary allusion to syphilis, of which Klimt was morbidly afraid. In one of the early preliminary studies which he himself published in *Ver Sacrum* in 1902, he took a man as a model (whereas the "emasculated" man of *Jurisprudence* derives from a woman, *She Who Was Once the Helmet-Maker's Beautiful Wife* by Rodin).

The child-woman with polymorphously perverse sexuality whose portrait Freud was to draw in *Drei Abhandlungen zur Sexualtheorie* (1905) reveals herself to be all the more disturbing because she is sufficient unto herself. Man has no place in the central panel. And the admirable *Water Snakes I* of 1904-1907, which turns the Lust of the frieze into two figures and provides a better explanation of her ecstatic sleep, formed the logical conclusion, in the same way that *Water Snakes II* reveals the real longings of the floating figures. The unveiled woman is the frightening revelation of a completely feminized universe.

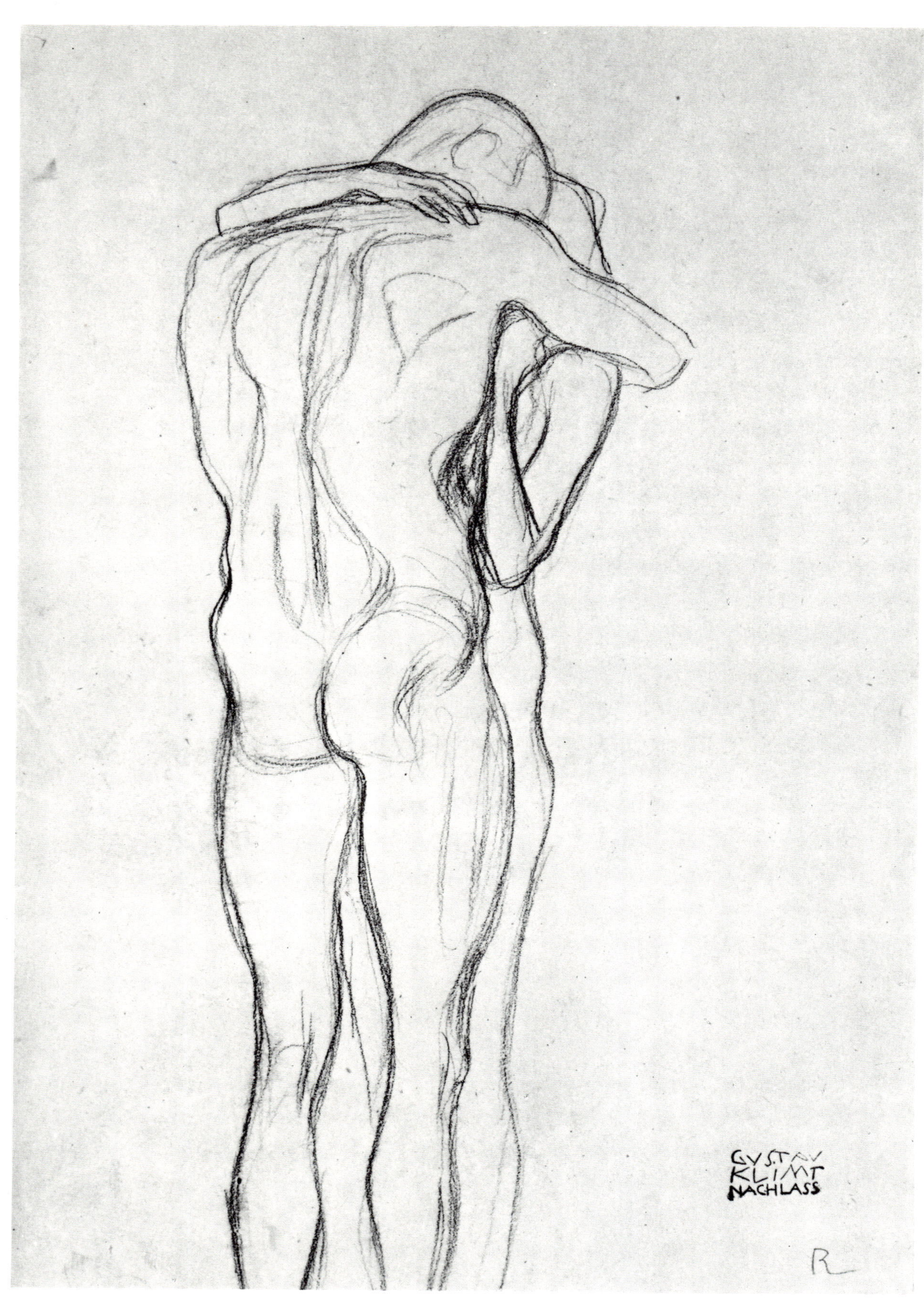

Gustav Klimt
Study for This Kiss for the Whole World. Black chalk.

The Beethovenesque "hero" then turns out to be in a very difficult position. Knight of the super-ego in the left-hand panel, his aggressive virility is cancelled out, after passing through the feminine filter of the Hostile Powers, by the idealized and evanescent Poetry on the right, a female figure placed in profile, like him, and at the same height. Naked and stripped of his armour, he displays in the Kiss an excessively athletic torso, with broad shoulders and muscles over-emphasized in relation to the surrounding flat surfaces, that makes it difficult genuinely to believe in his triumph. It is the woman's arms which imprison him and dominate his bent head, as Klimt was careful to point out more and more clearly in his beautiful preliminary studies. Unlike the Theseus in the 1898 poster who originally paraded a virility so flagrant that it caused the wrath of the censorship (and the insertion of a bush intended to render virility symbolically), his nudity now has nothing triumphant about it. With his feet caught in the waves (or veil?) uniting him with his companion (but not in her hair as the over-zealous interpretation of Carl E. Schorske, misled by old reproductions, would have it!), he is in exactly the same position of impotence as the old man in *Jurisprudence* before the castrating Furies. "Sexual ambiguity as punishment or fulfilment" (Schorske) does not put the two paintings in opposition to each other; it is already registered in its entirety in the frieze.

The hero begins in the womb formed by Ambition and Pity, as Carl E. Schorske has rightly observed, and completes his quest in the "belly" of another "womblike imprisonment" through which the flux of the cosmos runs. The final embrace is also a return to the beginning. If the woman is thus the true dominating figure, it is because she alone is in close union with the harmony of the world, as the splendid *Danae* of 1907-1908 proclaimed quite clearly. In it the masculine presence is reduced to the small black rectangle which we see passing close to her legs, carried along in the shower of gold, but it is the whole universe which gives the woman, alone and arched back on her "galactic" core, sexual satisfaction. The music which sustains the frieze is also the music of the spheres.

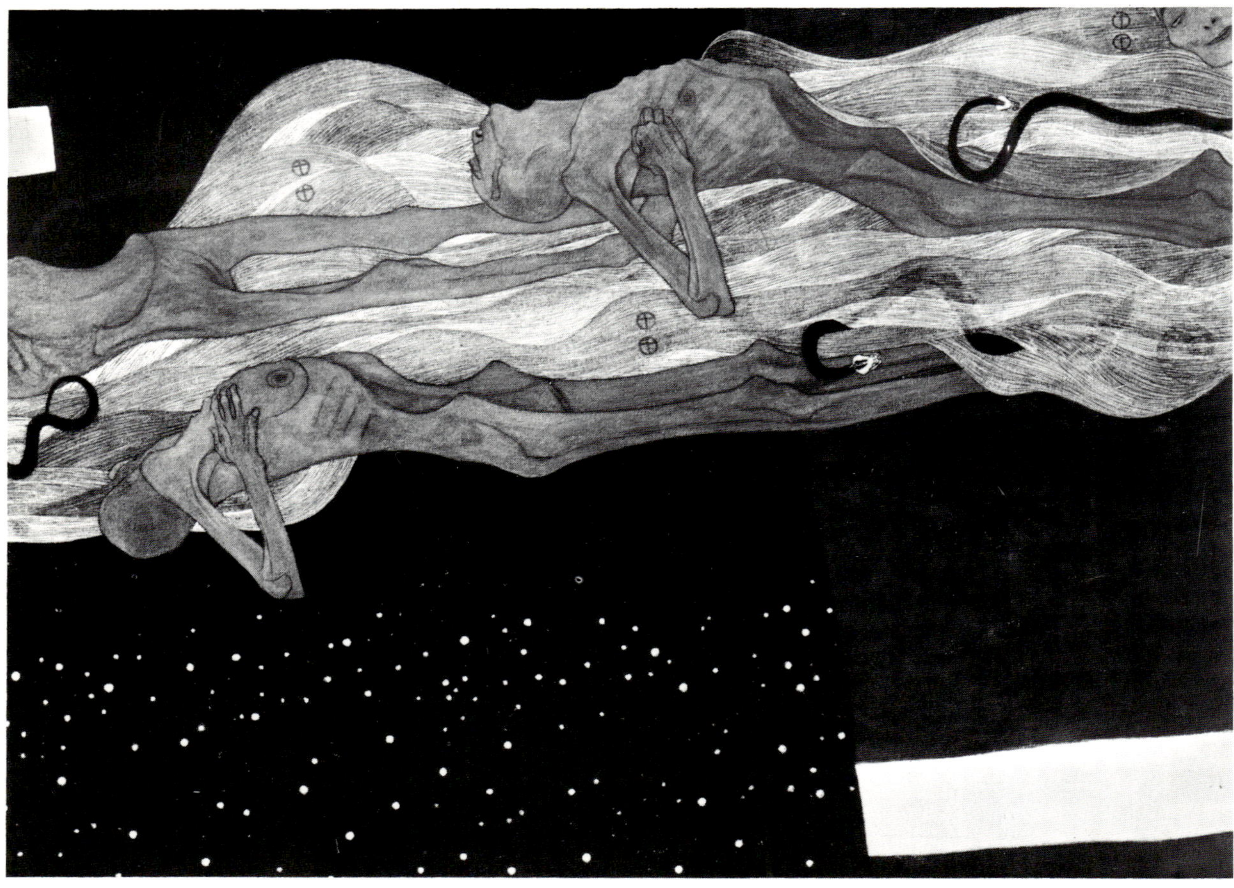

Gustav Klimt
The Procession of the Dead, 1903
(destroyed in 1945). Oil.

Even if the final kiss proclaims a new birth, Death (undoubtedly the figure with outspread arms above the Gorgons) also reigns in the central panel. The procession of figures floating from left to right soon afterwards turns into the extraordinary *Procession of the Dead* above the stars, from right to left (1903, destroyed in 1945), which, it has been suggested recently, should be placed vertically, although Klimt himself definitely had it reproduced horizontally (*Das Werk Gustav Klimts*, first edition, Vienna, 1914). Then we must return to Excess, more enigmatic than her two companions, in her caricatural appearance taken from Beardsley. Her embonpoint is a counterpart to the phthisis of Death. But above all she shows in profile that ballooning belly which is another Klimt leitmotiv. By a transfer comparable to that which led to the combination of *Music I* and *Music II*, the two images were to recur in closer association the following year in *Hope I*, another provocative work (Hartel persuaded Klimt not to show it at his 1903 retrospective) in which the death's heads, also placed in the upper part, are not so much the proclamation of a threat to the birth to come as the affirmation of an essential continuity. Harking back to the figure of the pregnant

Central panel: Heads of the Gorgons (below) and Sickness, Madness and Death (above).

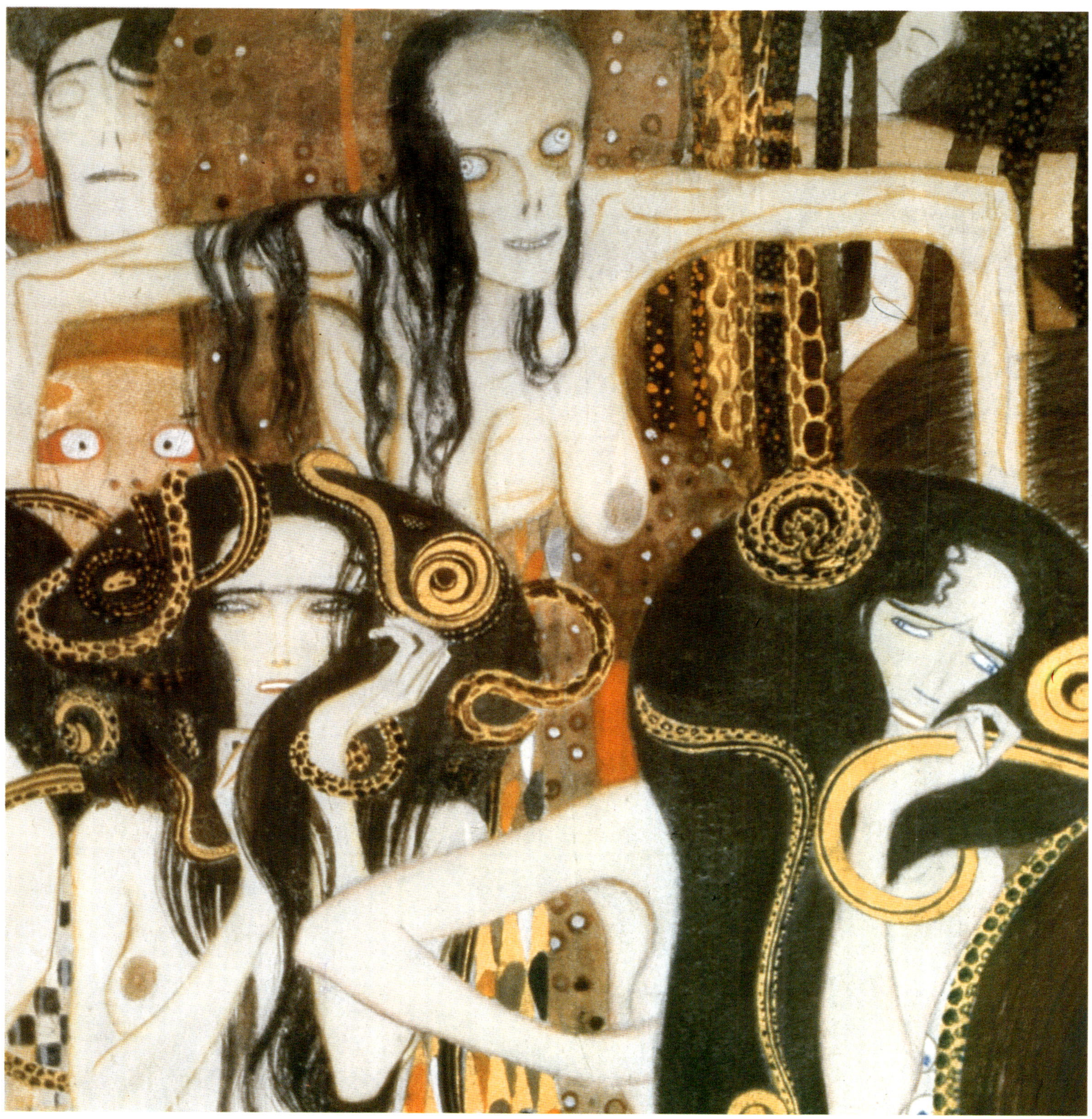

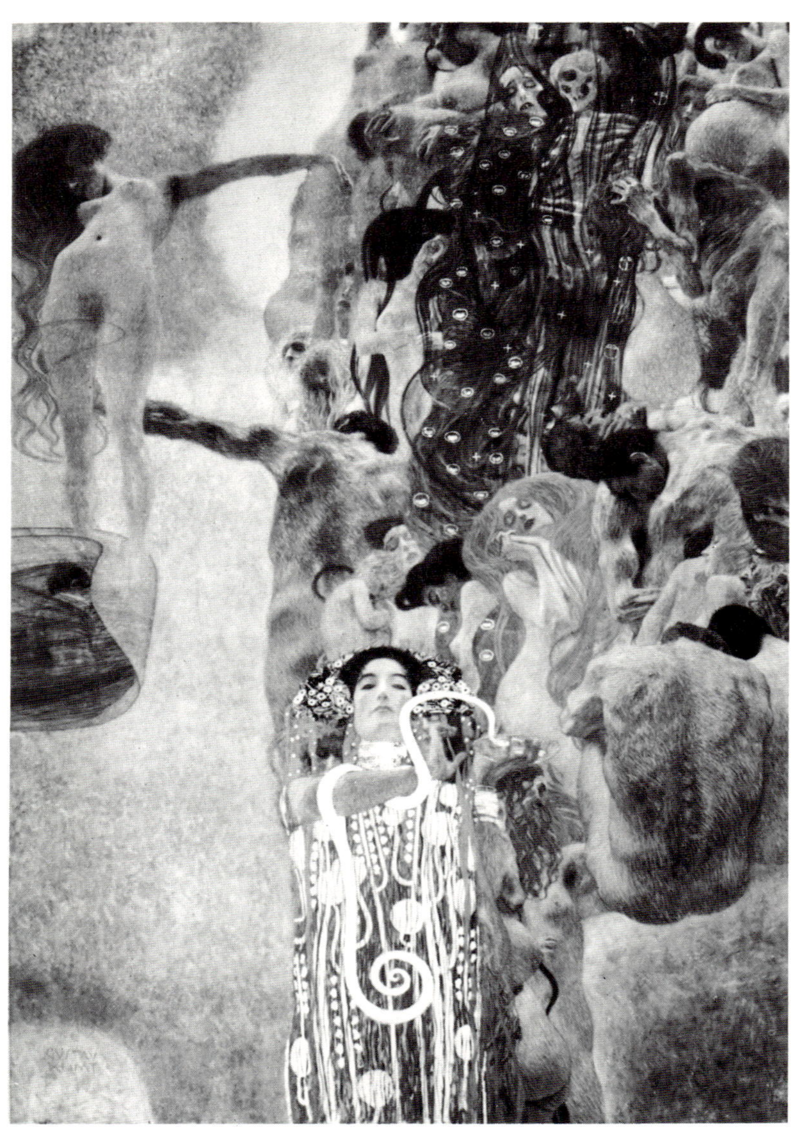

Gustav Klimt
Medicine, 1900-1901
(destroyed in 1945). Oil.

woman, the "negative" figure of Excess also reminds us that "lustful and perverse" woman is the bearer of life in her very sexuality. As for *Hope I*, it frames the frieze, as Life and Death frame Typhon, by replying to *Medicine* of 1900-1901 in which the same figure of a pregnant woman appeared at the top right, while Death draped in black led the procession of intertwined bodies with the escort of a large nude flaunting herself "lewdly"!

It is the watery (female) element which ensures the "bonding" in every sense of the word of this world engendered by the couple Eros-Thanatos, in particular the meaning attributed to it in "The Drunken Song" in *Thus Spake Zarathustra* ("All things are linked, enlaced, enamoured... All anew, eternally, all linked, enlaced, enamoured—ah, then ye *loved* the world... For *joy would have*

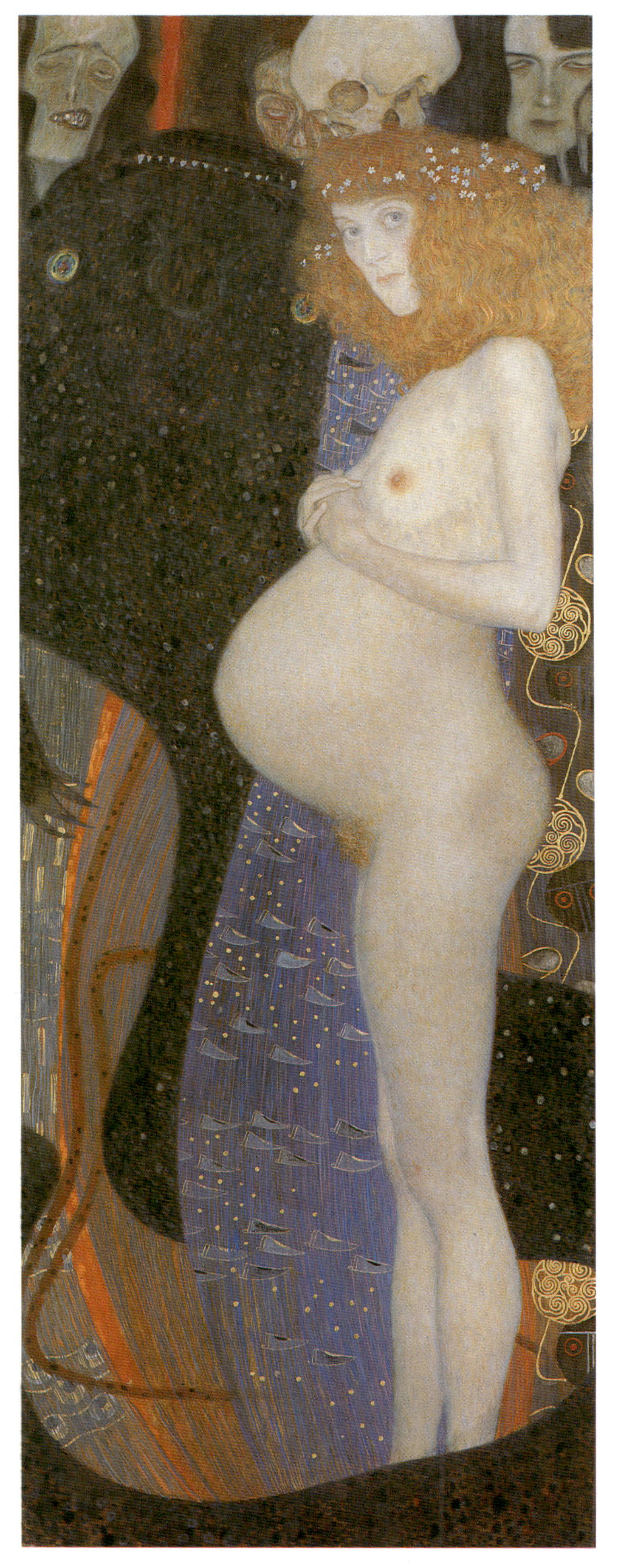

Gustav Klimt
Hope I, 1903. Oil.

eternity!"). It comes from the *blood* of *Fish Blood* drawn for *Ver Sacrum* in 1898 (with its flow of nymphs offering themselves, their long hair mingling with the current); it is moving towards the cloud of figures in the *Procession of the Dead* of 1903, by way of the linked undulating robes of the floating figures of the frieze and the long hair of the Arts, who are also immersed in the current, to culminate in the bluish swirl which, as in the *Nuda Veritas* of 1899, bathes the couple's feet. The snake which is associated with it in the last-named picture is also the serpent symbolizing the indissoluble union of life and death (its presence in Hygeia's arms in *Medicine* recalls the classical tradition on this subject). It recurs in the *Procession of the Dead* and the very title of *Water Snakes* in 1904-1907 is quite explicit in this respect. In the frieze it writhes in the Gorgons' hair and

Gustav Klimt
Fischblut ("Fish Blood"), drawing published in Ver Sacrum, *No. 3, 1898.*

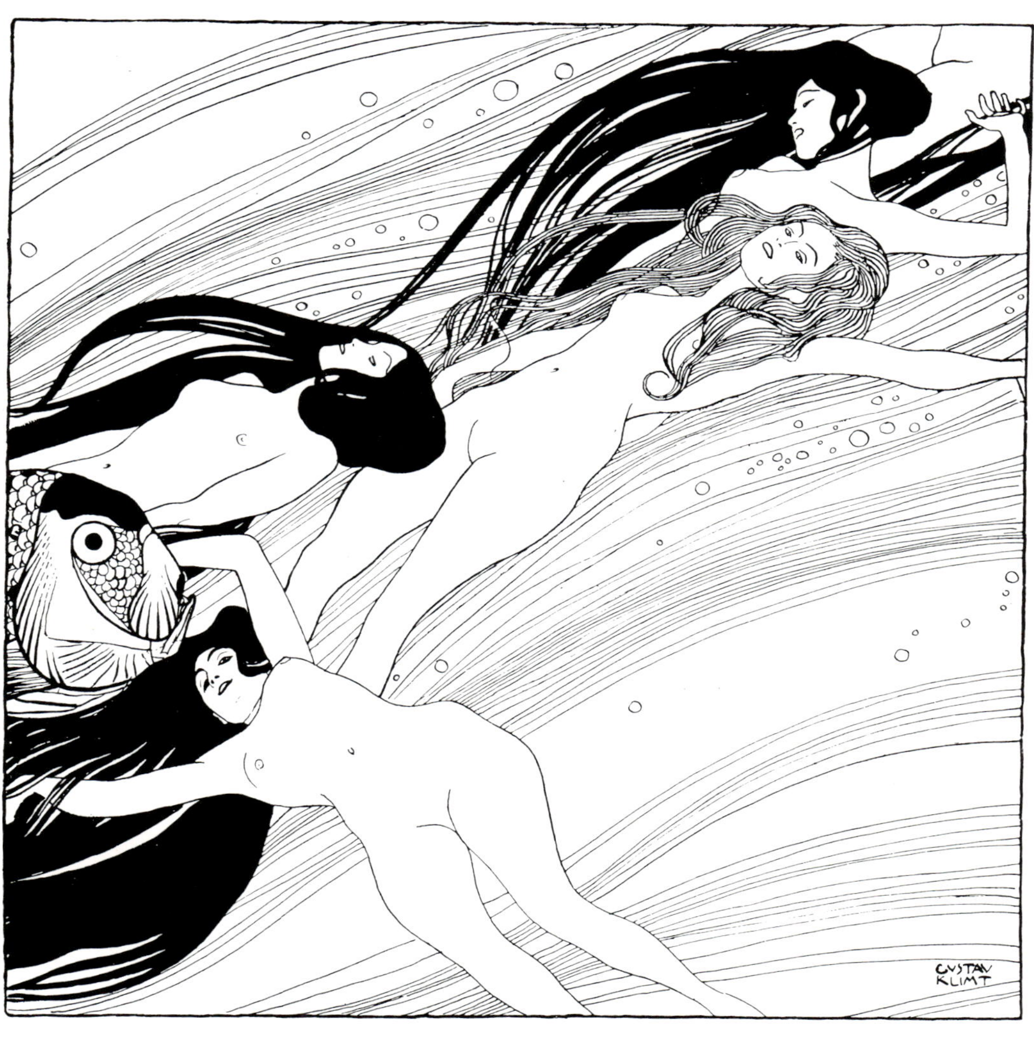

Right panel: The Arts.

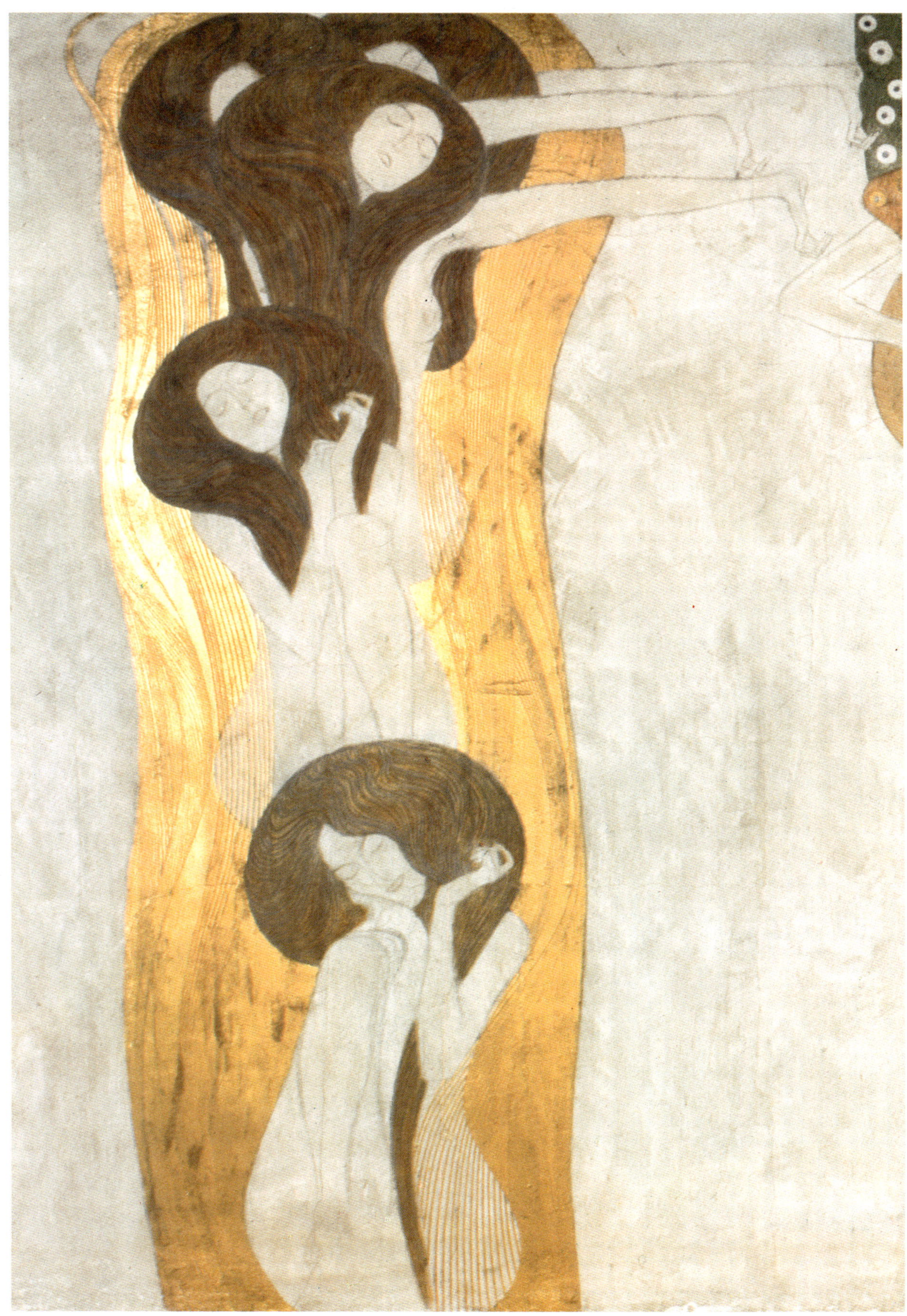

Gustav Klimt
Love, 1895. Oil.

in the actual tail of Typhon, whose lower body surrounded by vipers is mentioned in the ancient texts.

Thus once again there is a change from the rational mythology of his early works, the myth of armed victorious Athene still perpetuated in the same year, 1902, by Karl Kundmann's huge sculpture set up in front of the Viennese Parliament and to which everything in Klimt's work was now opposed.

There then remains the reply which the last scene tries to supply. This embrace by the hero, which is even more a return to the Paradise before birth, has hardly any relation to the fraternal Beethovenesque kiss. It replies at one and the same time, by diving further into the depths, to the *Love* of 1895 and to the twin Kisses of 1907-1908, one in the mosaic in the Palais Stoclet (entitled *Fulfilment*), the other the independent picture derived from it, *The Kiss*. The first-named introduced the series of erotic works by posing, below the disturbing presence of the heads in the upper part, the agonizing question of the kiss to come. The woman, a passive sphinx, withheld the answer that the frieze now tried to give. The malevolent figures have been pushed into the background in the central panel and do not flourish here any more than the stylized roses à la Mackintosh which have moved from the ornamental framework of *Love* to the Elysian garden surrounding the couple. This final rite is a rite of spring, no longer that of *Ver Sacrum* (which disappeared in 1903) nor Stravinsky's wild rite of 1913, but the vernal rite of the Viennese garden, the transformation of which during this period Carl E. Schorske has so remarkably analysed: "a garden strangely suspended between reality and utopia in which were expressed the self-satisfaction of those who knew what beauty was and their doubts about their social usefulness."

Klimt confirms and reinforces this interpretation when in 1903 he gives his new title to the final section of the frieze ("My Kingdom is not of this World") and even more when in his retrospective exhibition he places *next to it*, as a precious contemporary photograph shows, the *Nuda Veritas* of 1899 with the motto from Schiller which has replaced the epigraph by L. Schefer in the corresponding drawing published the previous year in *Ver Sacrum*. It serves to correct, if not to contradict, the "Kiss for the Whole World" of the

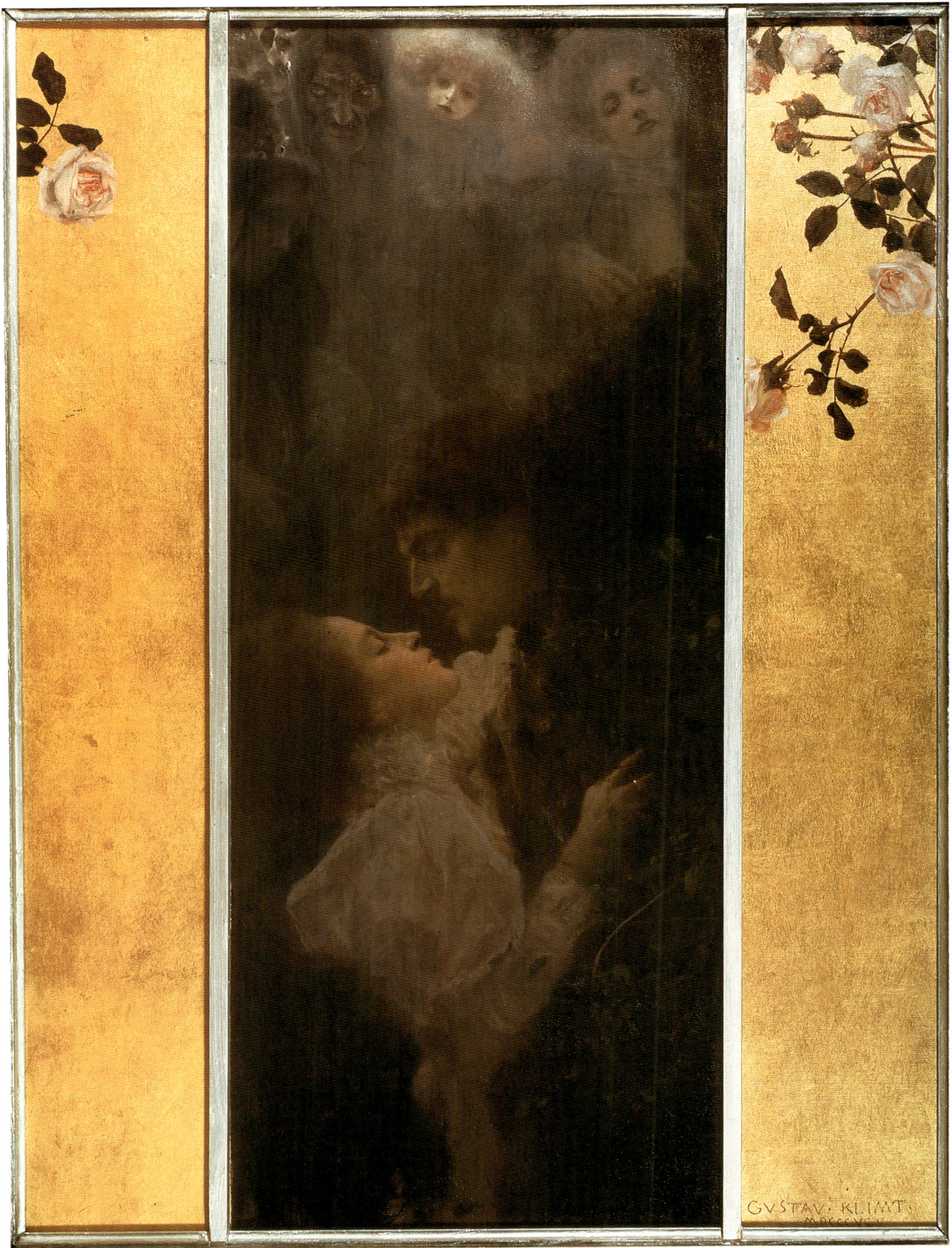
GVSTAV· KLIMT·

Gustav Klimt
Fulfilment, c. 1905-1909. Preparatory cartoon.

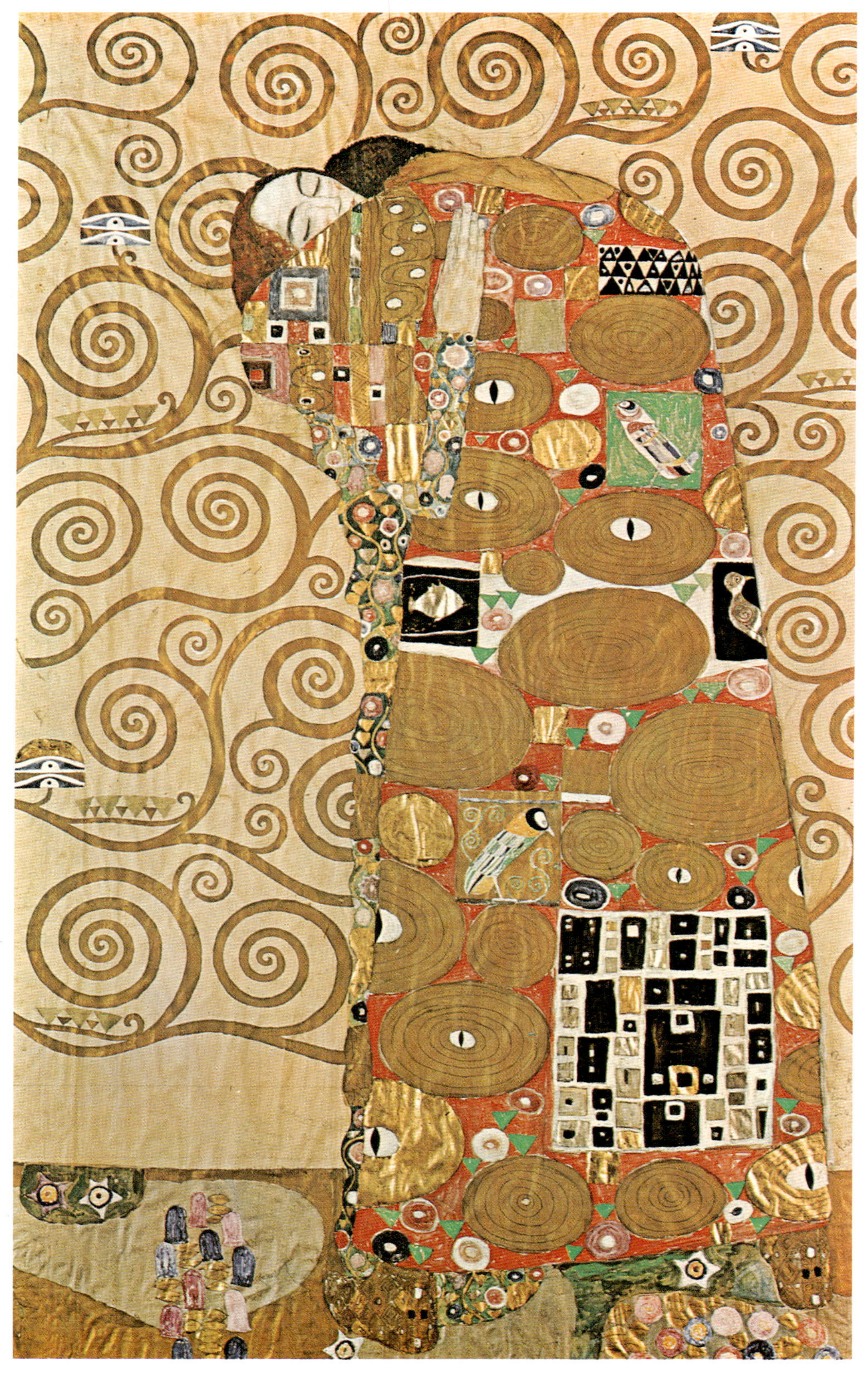

Gustav Klimt
The Kiss, 1907-1908. Oil.

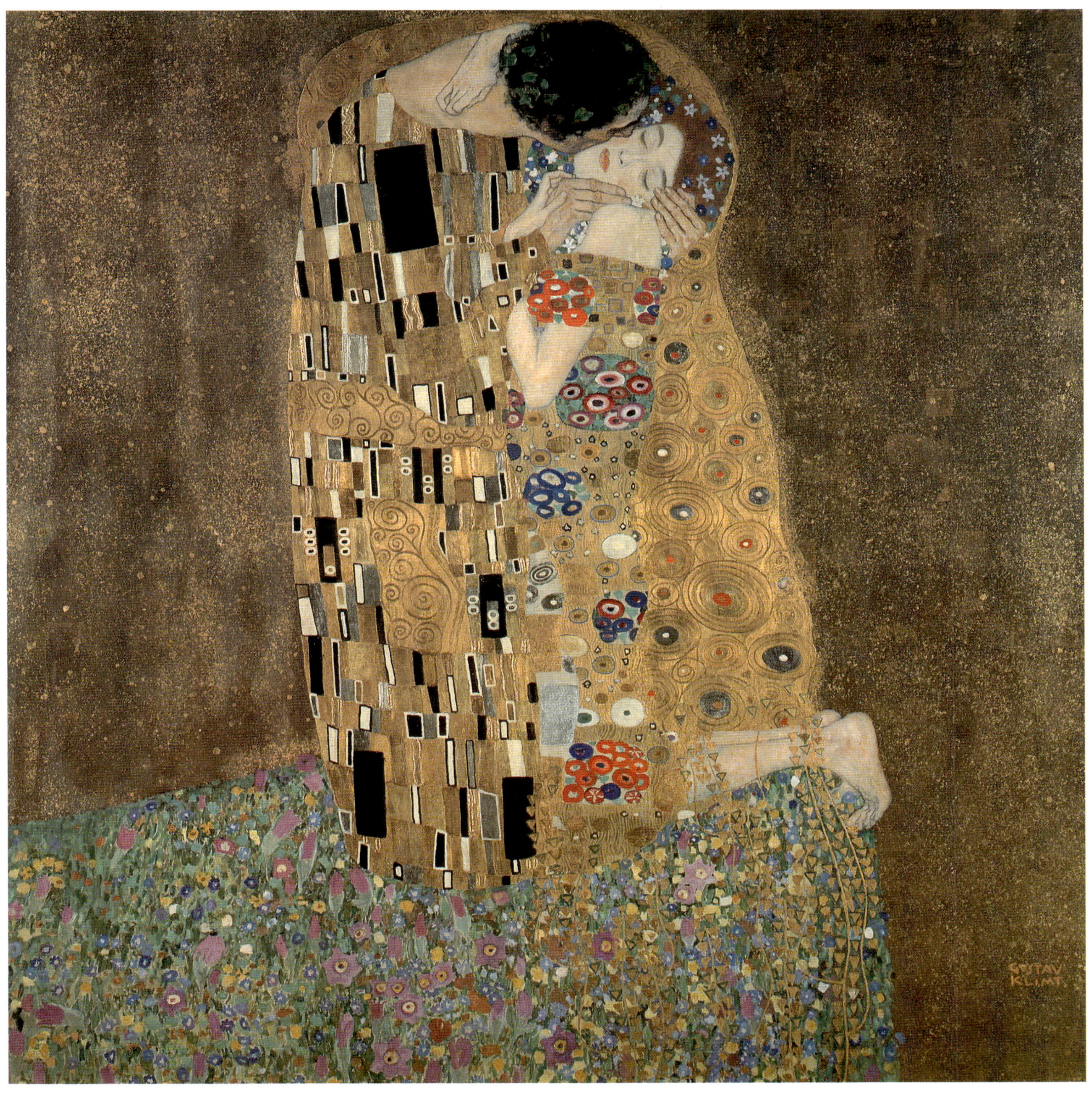

Right panel: This Kiss for the Whole World

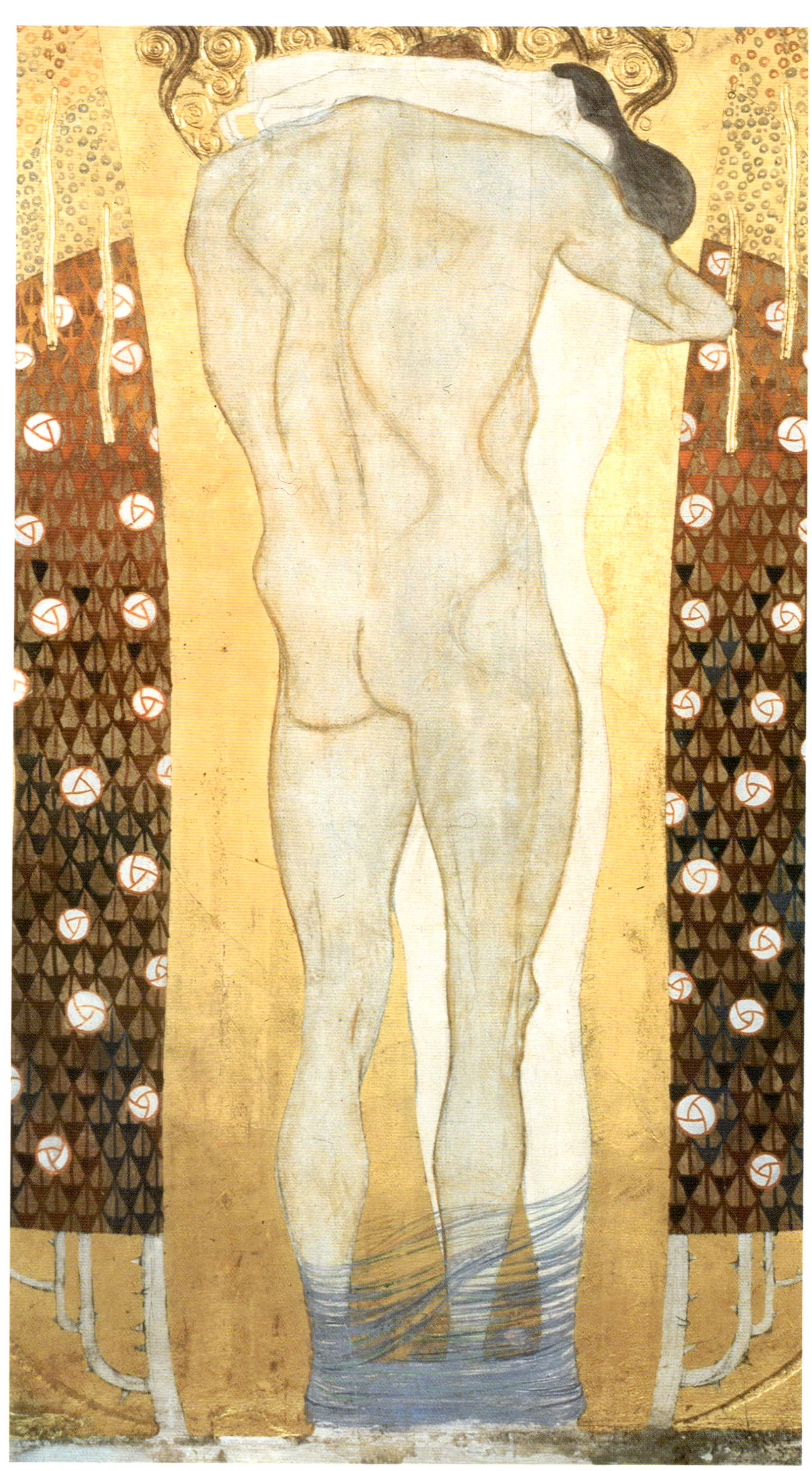

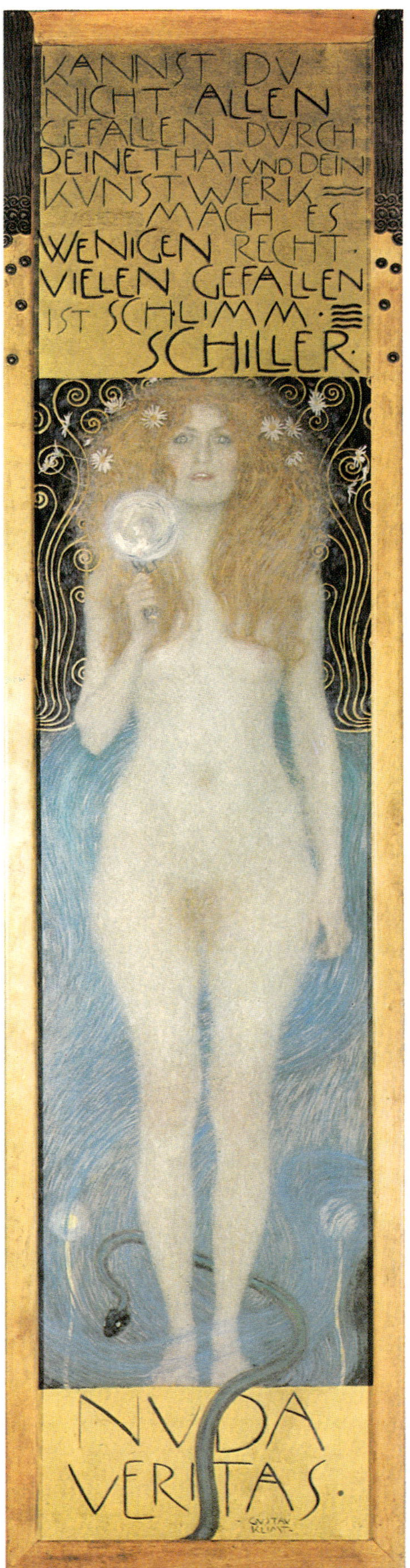

Gustav Klimt
Nuda Veritas, 1899. Oil.

Ode to Joy: "If you cannot please all by your actions and your art, make them suit the few. To please the many is bad." The *Millionen*, Beethoven's "millions of beings," are now only a happy few. And this *Nuda Veritas*, according to the apposite theory put forward by Carl E. Schorske, replies to the male nude of the frieze to rectify its significance. The garden, forming a flat surface like her, is really just another version of the "ornamented" dress in the contemporary portrait of Emilie Flöge. In the former, the body is in the garden (cf. the photographs of Emilie Flöge taken by Klimt in 1905), in the latter the "garden" is in the body.

The Stoclet "kisses" form the synthesis: not the "dressed" version of the kiss in the frieze, but once again a garden openly sexualized by the projection on to the "clothes" of the geometric male and female signs, of the body of the woman in her "fulfilment." Nevertheless, the Viennese garden was already disappearing: the first kiss had already taken refuge in Brussels, embedded in the mosaic of the Stoclet Palace, a "kingdom of the ideal" that had taken solidly material form. And that is also the significance of the transition from Art Nouveau to the art of the Wiener Werkstätte (Viennese Workshops) which were commissioned to execute the Stoclet decoration. In 1914 Kokoschka's *Bride of the Wind* also unites a couple, but in a chaotic, impossible love, carried away in the swirling eddies of a sea and a cloudy sky which offer an entirely different version of the cosmos. Now it is Alma Mahler, that "demoniacal" figure of Viennese sexuality, who is depicted next to the painter in the picture and inspires it, no longer Gustav, the "musician." The Viennese garden, the garden of Klimt and Emilie Flöge, has just exploded.

VI
Form

So it seems quite difficult to continue to interpret the frieze as straightforwardly as other art critics have done until now and explain it in terms that are purely psychological (sublimation and/or narcissistic regression) or sociological (the ideal of art as rejection of and refuge from the contemporary world). The revelation of sexuality in its frightening dimension as the driving force of the world, prevents us *a fortiori* from speaking of a work procuring "evasion and consolation" (Carl E. Schorske). But faced with this void traversed by disturbing figures that he has just unveiled, it is true that the painter's only salvation is in the actual *existence* of art. And that is where Klimt once again rejoins Freud, from whom he separated himself by renouncing the celebration of the triumph of Athene over the powers of repression, instinct and darkness. "Art, that path to freedom from sexual servitudes, has its origin in these powers. The artist gives form to his phantasms and desires according to aesthetic rules... so the appreciation of aesthetic forms which he provokes is tantamount to a reordering of the disordered and indefinite world of primitive sexuality" (*Das Interesse an der Psychoanalyse*, 1913). Sublimation by art, and, vice versa, its extreme sexualization are not the subject of an exposition in the order of the *representation*, but they are exhibited in its production, in art itself. And the "underlying" or "hidden" meaning of the frieze is not to be sought in this complicated montage, this fascinating fabric which iconographic and thematic analyses keep on revealing. If it carries with it the accepted concepts of the cultural context or those of a particular psychological structure, it is to reinstate and then redeploy them on the expanse of the wall and its *surfaces*.

This is perhaps where the second Wagnerian interpretation of Beethoven's work recurs. I refer to Wagner's 1870 essay, which, unlike the "program" of 1846, formalizes the Ninth Symphony to the point of denying its *words* any real importance ("It is not the lines of the poet who wrote the text which can determine the music, whether he be Goethe or Schiller; it is the drama alone which has this power and I do not mean by that the dramatic poem, but the drama which is actually unfolding before our eyes..."). That is his most valuable legacy: "It is not Beethoven's work, but the unprecedented artistic act it encloses that we have to retain... the most perfect artistic form, that form in which every conventional character would be totally suppressed, not only for the drama, but also and especially for the music." For Wagner that means above all rejection of the sonata form, purely rational and of wholly external origin, opposed to the continuity of the Beethovenesque "melody" (in Opus 131 in particular) in which "each part of the accompaniment, each rhythmic sign and even silence" play their part. Thus, at a crucial moment, Wagner's essay ranks high in the original Art Nouveau statements of intent which rejected the "fashion" of historicist styles to show that the total work of art would not emerge from the mutual imitation of the arts but from the "coinciding" of the specific treatment of their form (as Beethoven's world "corresponds" to Shakespeare's in the *Overture to Coriolanus*, for example). Henry van de Velde was to express the same distinction forcefully in his book *Déblaiement d'Art* (Clearing Up Art) in 1894. And it is to this fundamental theme that Klinger's text, reprinted in the catalogue of the 1902 exhibition, returns when he quotes Wagner.

This is the very moment when Klimt makes use of the legacy of the pictorial avant-gardes who preceded him in this field and formalizes his painting, but in his case under the sign or *signs* of sexuality (portrait of Emilie Flöge). Before being the formulation of a program, the frieze is an occupation of space and the form this takes quite as much as the thematic content helps to displace if not cancel the original programmatic concept.

That is why it is idle to seek to enumerate its multiple sources, which, even when added together, could never lead to the final result. They include Mackintosh (for the linearity, the bell shapes, the rosebush of the kiss), Toorop (for the floating figures and many stylizations, notably in the treatment of hair), Minne (for the emaciated figures of Suffering Humanity and Care), Hodler (for the parallelisms, especially in the choir of angels), Rodin, Khnopff, Beardsley, and why not Puvis de Chavannes, and most of all the Nabis, whom Germanic and Anglo-Saxon writers forget, not to mention the Assyrian, Egyptian and Byzantine references which critics immediately seized on and which are evident in the arrangement of the figures and certain details of the ornamentation. Vienna at the time was by definition a melting-pot which is also exemplified

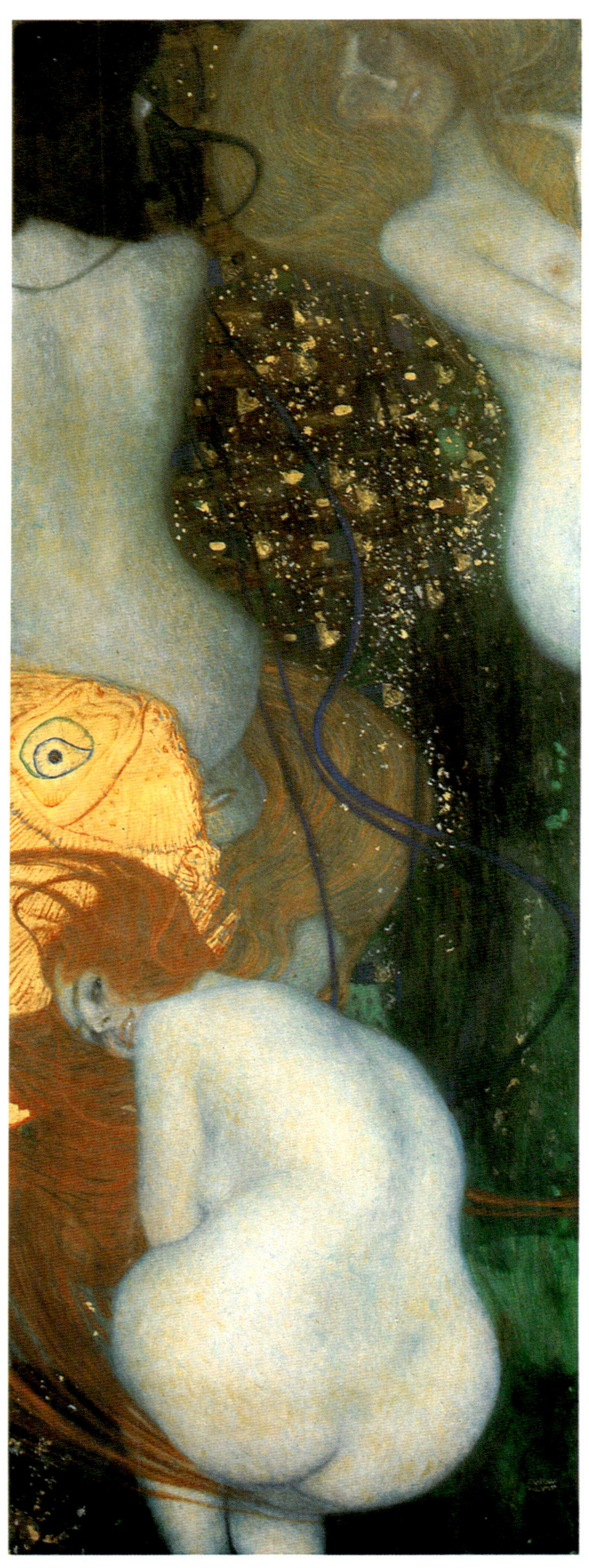

Gustav Klimt
Goldfish, 1901-1902. Oil.

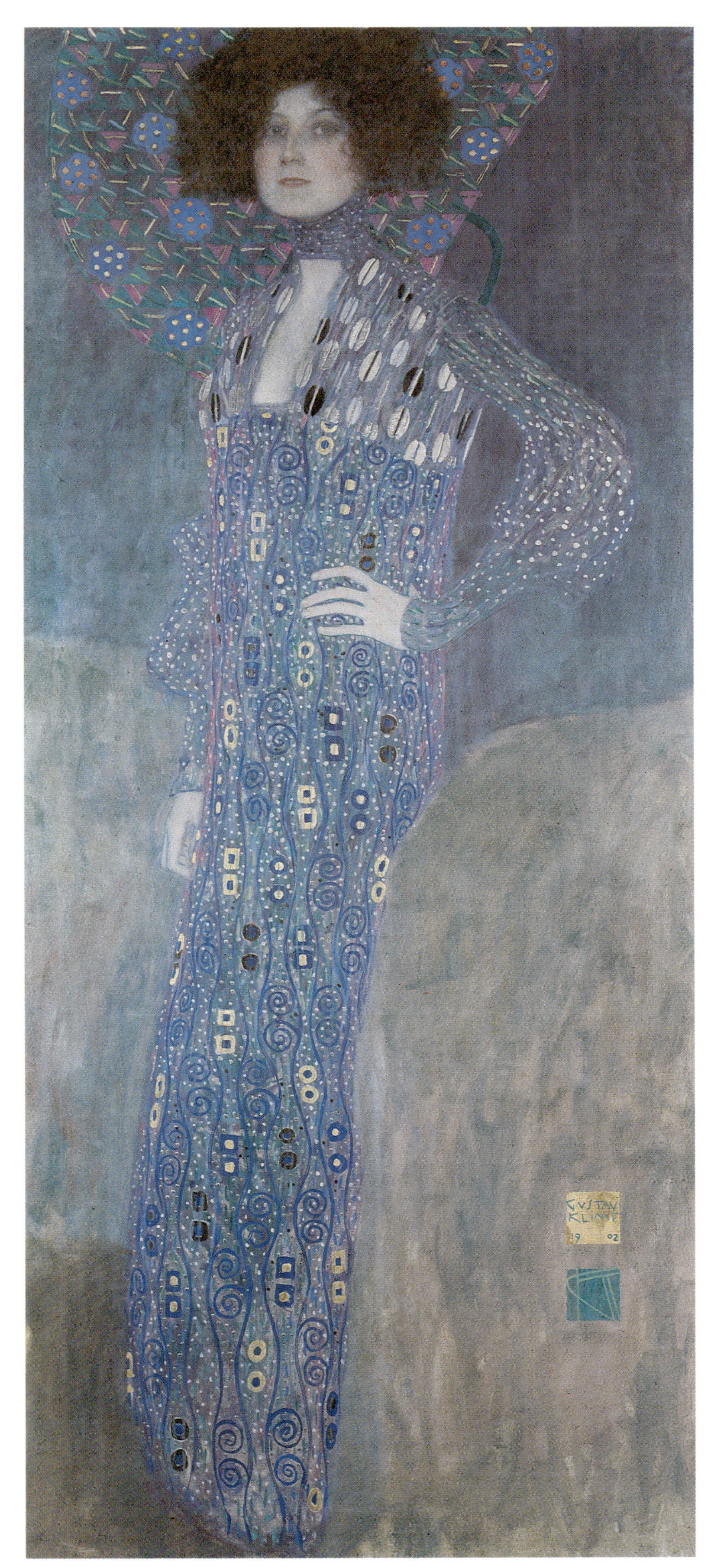

Gustav Klimt
Portrait of Emilie Flöge, 1902. Oil.

Gustav Klimt
Study for the central and left Gorgons. Black chalk.

by the contemporary literature of *Jung Wien* and its multiple mirror effects.

This placing in space begins with the tripartition already mentioned, which, by the "loading" of the richer, denser and darker central panel, contradicts from the start the alleged progression of the narrative. The effects of inherent flatness and asymmetry then work on this continuous band. The earlier parts, which ensure cohesion with the architecture, show up more subtly the contrast between the strict idealizing flat surfaces and the suggestions of volume (in the muscular body of the hero, for example, shown three-quarters length into the bargain). The volume, being more "external," approaches the reality of the world, but equally distances itself from the reality of the frieze, of the wall, of art. In the same way the nude in the foreground of *Goldfish*, a sarcastic work, "breaks" the surface of the picture to annoy the critics incapable of entering the world of art, whereas Emilie Flöge's much more erotic dress contains it in the materiality of the surface alone. But conversely the effect of relief is reinforced by a technique of scraping the ground which brings out the darker parts and gives the effect of a "negative" which preserves the coherence of the whole.

The asymmetry, of remote Japanese influence, decentres each of the panels, introducing caesuras and musical intervals, which correspond in effect to the Beethovenesque "melody" as presented by Wagner.

Silence (the blank space between Poetry and the Arts) finds a place there, as do the "rhythmic signs" (the floating figures, repeated identically, but in differing numbers). Like the varying importance attached to different developments in Opus 131, the dislocation of what ought to be a regular rational arrangement is done for the benefit of the greater organic unity of the whole. Around the two pivots of the Knight and Poetry, placed off-centre on their respective walls but facing each other, the final group with its serried ranks of the Arts and angels at the end of the frieze seeks to counterbalance the compact panel of the Hostile Powers, themselves pushed to the left. This is a slanting axis which crosses the axis that the room itself forms with the Klinger statue at right angles... This interlocking of off-centre elements, quite as daring as the

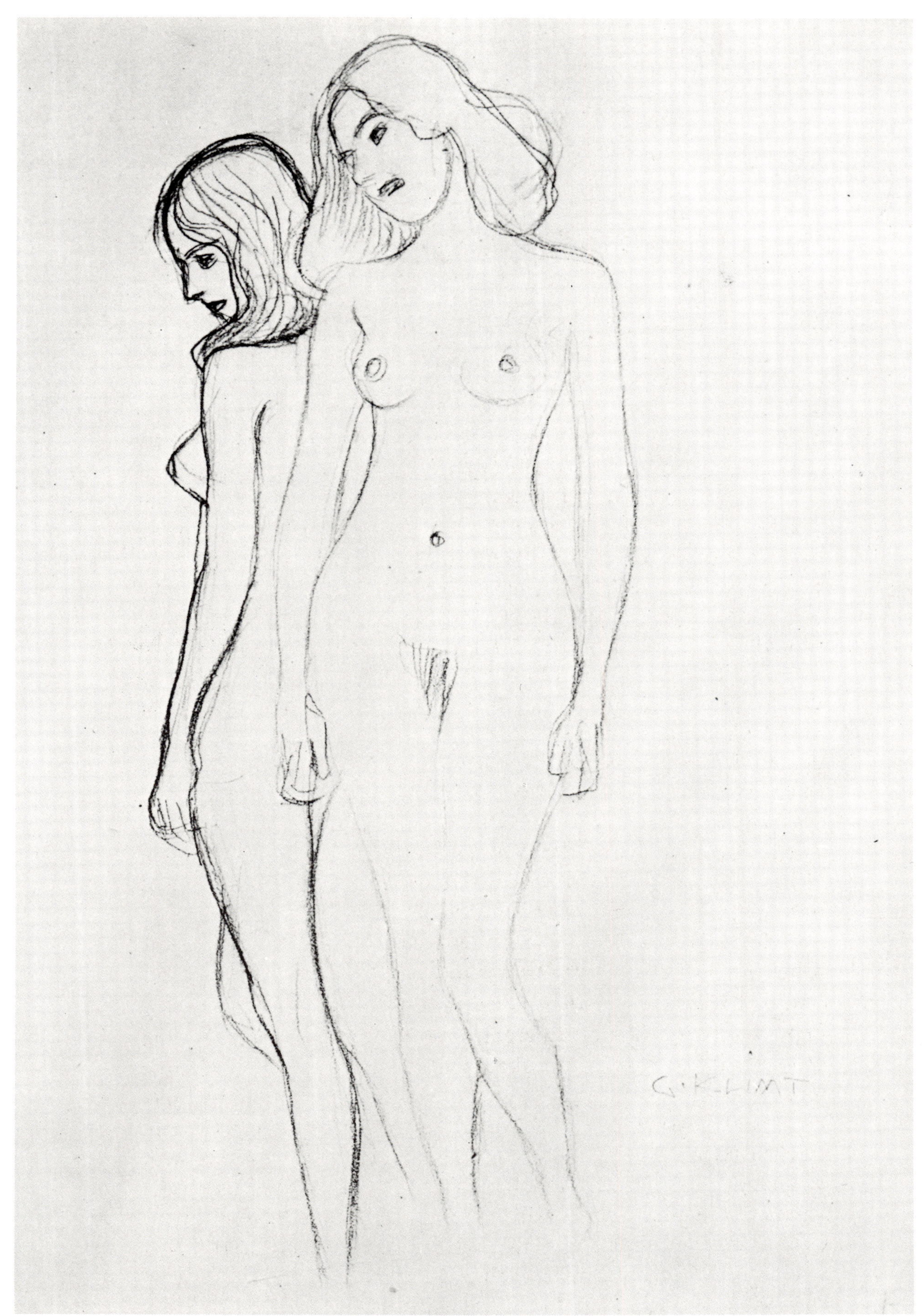
G. KLIMT

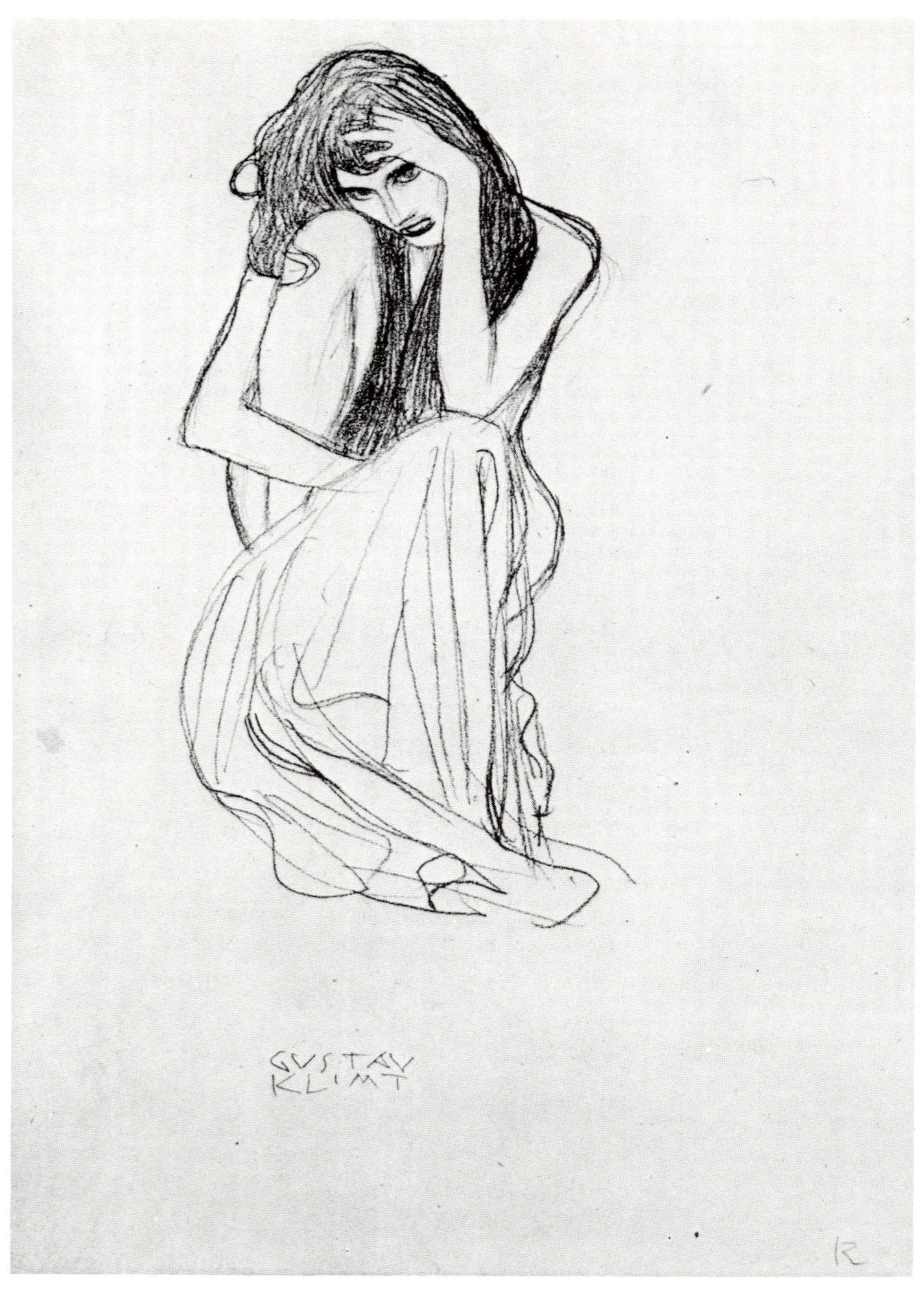

Gustav Klimt
Study for Nagging Care. Black chalk.

"amorphous" spaces of the University panels, works against what should be the linear dynamism of the "narrative." Here, too, the "words" matter less than the "music," which should normally do no more than accompany them.

As for the actual "figures," the systematic stylization to which they are subject starting from an expressive pose, already tending to reduce them to a simple sign (the "S" of the withdrawal into the self, the hook of faces cut off and resting on the shoulder, the linked up curves) can be read particularly well in the some 120 preliminary studies still extant. But most important is surely that "invention of signs" to which it leads and which Klimt's later work accentuated still further.

In the centre, the decisive element: the original Art Nouveau arabesque, the living line as a force which Van de Velde sought in the movement of wind, fire and water, but whose real anchorage Klimt finds in the centre of the female figure of Lewdness, central figure and cleft of the frieze where the line of her hair and thighs prolongs and links up with, above and below, the line of the hirsute bestiality of the monster, beyond the bisexual snakes... Embryonic coils, nodal vibration in the original sense of the term, conceived as matrix of the work. The eroticization of art which becomes art itself and, unlike the obscenity of Rops with which it parts company, founds the practice of a way of painting.

Around, the gravitational pull of the secondary signs which derive from it: female triangles, spirals and ocelli, male squares and rectangles, projecting on to the whole the fundamental contrast which translates plastically the very essence of the world. Later, geometric abstraction provided its puritan version, which was transposed if not travestied when deprived of the "lewd" arabesque which is nevertheless its true source.

And the three primary colours (blue, yellow and red) also reunited in the three figures of the central group finally complete this vocabulary of an "elementalism" which is surely based on other foundations than Van Doesburg's or Moholy-Nagy's.

Unlike the image and the symbol, the sign remains open and makes no claim to lead to another "underlying" reality: it is a work of return to the surface, the opposite, at this point, as Alessandra Comini has rightly emphasized, of the Freudian approach. Just like the *Kiss* by Munch and the one by Behrens, which were more or less contemporary, Klimt's *Kiss* is primarily an embrace of lines. With its opposing curve and uprights, the painter's new monogram signs and sums up the formalized omnipresence of Eros. It is also significant that it appears below his former signature in the portrait of Emilie Flöge.

Thus, founded on a dialectic between the male/female sign, creating form then rests on the key idea and systematic handling of contrasts. In the image, the contrasts between realism and the ideal, frontality and profile, movement and immobility. In the foreground, contrast between occupied spaces and voids, light and dark, agitated parts and calm areas, supple lines and broken outlines, verticals and horizontals, descriptive and transfiguring colours. In the material, contrasts of traditional techniques as opposed to gilding, rough plaster and numerous inlays with semi-precious materials (pearl, mother-of-pearl) or prosaic ones (curtain rings, upholstery tacks, buttons, bits of broken mirrors, especially in Excess). Lastly in the treatment, contrast in the different handling of surfaces: hollows and reliefs, different techniques of scratching the ground (with the resultant effects of matness or glossiness), opposition of textures (the rough body of Typhon against the smooth bodies of the trio of Lewdness).

But the most important thing is that, as with Beethoven, a point which Wagner takes great care to emphasize, the notion of contrast alone is responsible for providing the meaning. The undisguised truth of the materials (another central Art Nouveau theme), which is also the truth of surface appearances, equally serves to show up the ostensible truth of the "contents." *Truth* is naked (allegory), but her mirror reflects only the mother-of-pearl of her skin. All this produces the perpetual opposition of contrasts which are so many denials of an over-explicit meaning. The Arts, for example, are made of a light material, like transparent ether, but their drawing, the long voluptuous curving profusely repeated line surrounding them, and their actual pose relate back to the sensual presence of Lewdness and Lust. Although Poetry is drawn in an extremely idealized way, she has a dress and a lyre ornamented with pearls and rich relief gilding which are quite as sumptuous as the coiffure and belt of Excess. The reclining figures already share the same ecstasy as the Arts and the Heavenly Angels, but their gilded flower-filled hair carries echoes of Lewdness and Lust, herself curled back and withdrawn into her selfish pleasure, as Pity is wrapped up in her own feeling of emotion.

So the "true" contrast is ultimately the conveyor of ambiguity; it blurs the tracks, cancelling out one effect by another and reversing the meaning so that in the end its own truth to itself is the winner. The symbolism is shown up, or reversed, the themes are completely exposed. Projection on to the wall, in real space, is by itself the unveiling of the meaning. Like music, which for Wagner in 1870 "does not represent the Ideas contained in the phenomena of the world, but is itself an Idea of the world, even a total idea," Art Nouveau painting in the final phase which brought Klimt and Hodler

Left panel: Heads of the Knight in Armour, Ambition and Pity.

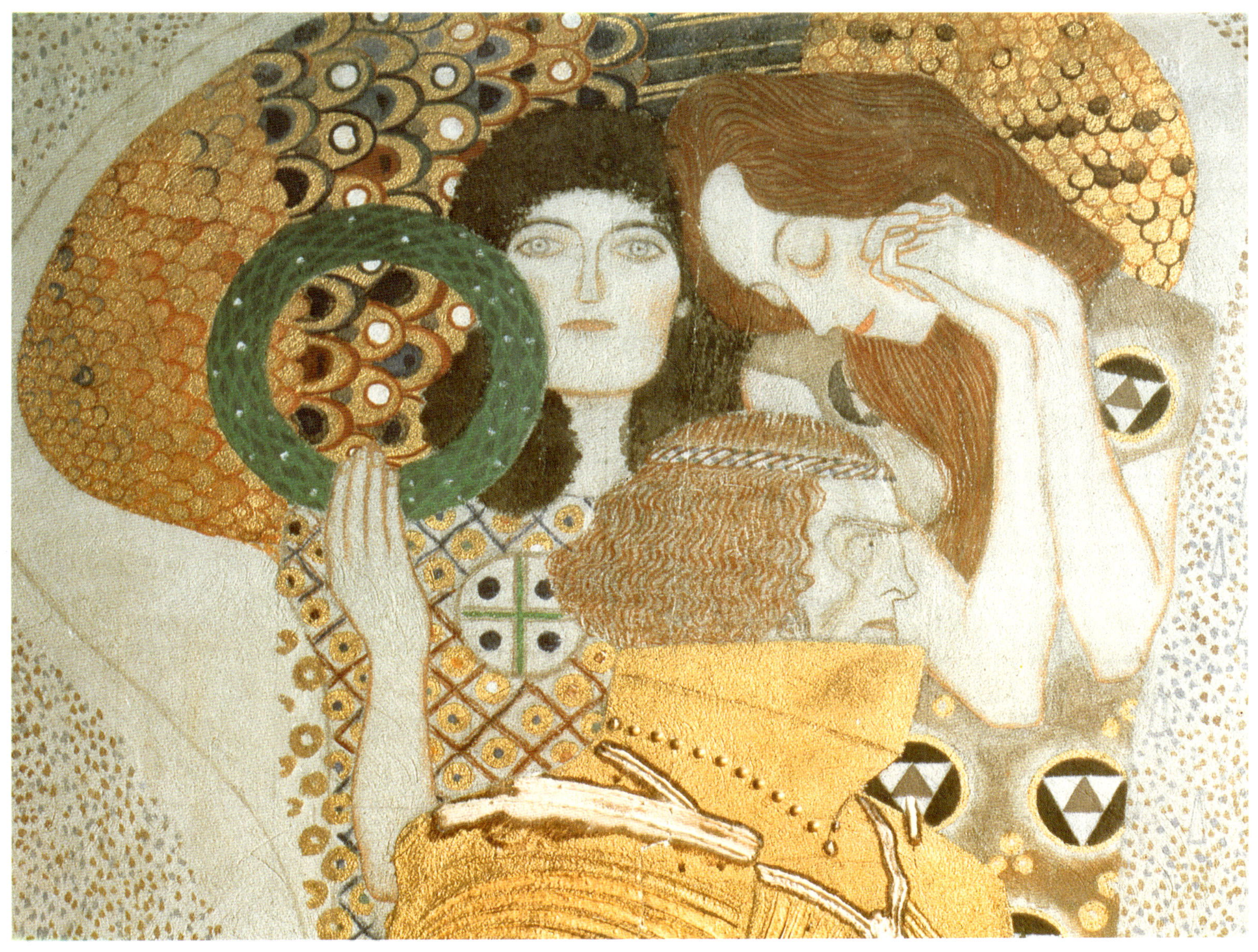

together in Vienna exposes its whole content in its form. That is the meaning of its "decorative" conversion which conceals no snare or reductive constraint and does not necessarily imply loss of contact with the real (Schorske). It is in 1902 that Klimt finally finds his artistic way and his freedom, after what was already a long and rich career.

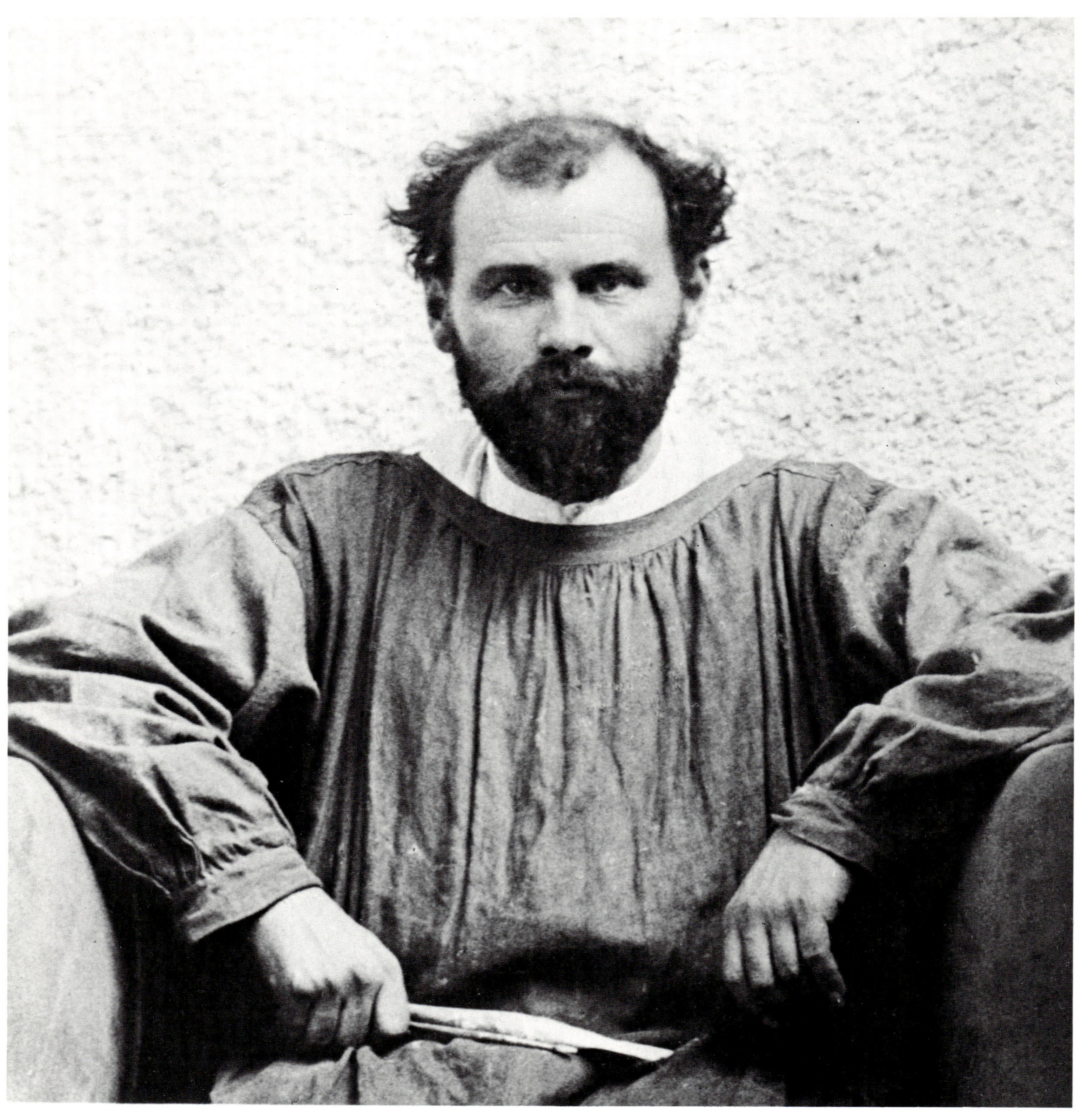

Photograph of Klimt at the Beethoven Exhibition, 1902.

VII
Synthesis

In the Beethoven Frieze form conveys the meaning even more than the association of motifs and themes. But Klimt, who refused to comment on his work, read little and was rather taciturn, felt that this form which spoke for itself should remain open. To the challenge implicit in the motto inscribed on the Secession building ("To every age its Art, to Art its freedom"), the frieze does not give a straightforward answer. Was it a work of defiance just when the harshest attacks were being made on the immense effort undertaken by Klimt on the University panels? A work of "readjustment of the ego" when a world vision hitherto based too exclusively on the enlightenment of Athene and the suppression of the Minotaur in the darkness of the labyrinth was collapsing? Of course, but still not a work of egoistic withdrawal, of regression into the "narcissistic" and "aesthetic-cum-erotic Utopia" (Schorske). Admittedly the (false) triumph of the hero in the final scene is no longer the triumph of the super-ego, but neither is it evidence of taking refuge in the garden of delights. Even if the Kiss puts into practice Schiller's advice chosen as motto for the *Nuda Veritas* of 1899, it still does not give a "closed" answer. The (excessively) regular arrangement of the garden is traversed by long arabesques which link it with the whole of the cosmos and hark back to her who in the central panel denotes the Origin, because the *hortus conclusus* opens on to the whole world of forms, wholly permeated by original sexuality. Klimt's narcissism (cf. the Lesbians in *Water Snakes*) only turns away from the immediate accidental world the better to dive back into the primitive current which is birth, end and eternity of the world. That is the revelation made to Narcissus by the mirror (water) of Truth over which he leans. Thus it links up (remarkably enough in much the same terms) with the narcissism whose rarefied philosophy Hugo von Hofmannsthal expounded in the letters written to his friend Edgar Freiherr von Bebenburg in 1895: "I should like to feel the being of all things strongly and to be plunged in being so as to feel its true deep meaning. For the whole universe is full of meaning, meaning that has become form... The words are not of this world, they are a world apart and of itself, a world quite as complete as the world of sounds... If one falls in love with oneself and if, like Narcissus, one falls into the water, I think that that is the moment when one is about to fall headlong down into the right way... 'In love with oneself,' I mean to say with life, or God, as you will."

So there is some relevance in returning to sociological interpretations. In spite of the Körber government's attempts to achieve cultural consolidation in Vienna, it was obvious that the frieze was not really a work of "integration" in the existing conditions. The assertion of the omnipotence of sexuality would have been enough to identify it as breaking with and outside this process, as Klimt himself henceforth was. The violent reactions of the public and many of the critics clearly confirm this. Depending on their point of view, all it represented was a "theatre of pagan orgies," a panopticon of venereal diseases (referring to a waxwork show in the Prater, the Präuscher Panoptikum), "frescoes better suited to a temple of Krafft-Ebing," "rickety and tubercular" or "voluptuous and spongy" harlots (the *Salzburger Volksblatt*), "Assyrian bagnios," etc. The exhibition had a *succès de scandale* (and with more than 58,000 visitors even enabled the Secession to make a profit), but the only admiration came from friends, such as Ludwig Hevesi, who called the frieze Klimt's masterpiece, and Rodin who came to Vienna soon afterwards and who, according to a witness, complimented Klimt on a frieze that was "so tragic and so blissful" (*so tragisch und so selig*).

In spite of these words of praise, the work was obviously destined for oblivion and its survival after the 1903 Klimt retrospective was only due to two friends and patrons, first Carl Reininghaus and then August Lederer. The latter acquired it in 1918 through the intermediary of Egon Schiele. (From the Lederer family it was bought by the Austrian government in 1973 and finally restored in 1985.) It had never been genuinely accepted by and even less integrated with the political and social climate in which it appeared. It also marks Klimt's renunciation of the search for a mythical "Austrian art" to rejoin (witness the admiration of Rodin and Hodler, who used the central Gorgon for his *Truth II* of 1903) the avant-garde of international Art Nouveau.

More seriously, Klimt aroused the opposition of a new Viennese avant-garde which had Adolf Loos and Karl Kraus as two of its most forceful spokesmen. Indeed it was the actual program of the

Secession (and of Klimt in particular) which Loos challenged when he denounced the attempt to integrate the arts and the use of ornament to remodel society in terms of aesthetics. It is typical (but has it been duly noticed?) that in Loos's most famous utterance on this subject, *Ornament and Crime* (1908), the Ninth Symphony recurs as a leitmotiv in a probable reference to Klimt and the 1902 frieze: "All art is erotic. The first ornament that was born, the cross, was of erotic origin... A horizontal line: the recumbent woman. A vertical line: the man penetrating her. The man who created that felt the same impulse as Beethoven when he created the Ninth Symphony. But the man of our time who from an inner compulsion smears walls with erotic symbols is a criminal or a degenerate... Just as ornament is no longer organically linked with our culture, so it is also no longer an expression of our culture... It is in no way attached to the order of the world... The Ninth Symphony could never have been composed by a man forced to wear silk, satin and lace. Today the man who appears in public dressed in velvet is not an artist, but a buffoon or a dauber!"

Apart from the possible allusion to the celebrated tunics Klimt wore (especially when he was working on the frieze), Loos, by separating the beautiful from the useful, by extolling a "private" art of revolt on the one hand, and a "social" architecture of acceptance of the real on the other, claims to denounce another hypocrisy which would be a new "travesty" of reality. When he called for a return to the separation of the arts, he blew the ideology of Art Nouveau to bits and inaugurated the Expressionist phase of the "explosion of the garden" which, with Kokoschka, Trakl and Schönberg as its leading figures, did not end, after the intervening cataclysm of war, until the early 1920s when a new Utopia was formed. But in so doing and with this "vulgarization" of an *eroticism* judged out of date which contradicted what Freud said at the time about the topicality of *sexuality*, Loos expresses in the clearest, most explicit terms the fundamental misunderstanding which Klimt's painting had to suffer for so long.

That applies equally to Karl Kraus when he pleads against Klimt's *Philosophy* in 1900, demanding that the choice of allegories (a principle Klimt was already abandoning) be entrusted to the "specialists" of knowledge, the philosophers themselves.

Klimt's "conservative revolution" (Werner Hofmann) was thus doubly in danger. Eluding the dialectic of the avant-gardes (which, according to classic Marxist theory, ought to lead to their progressive integration with the body social), its only recourse was to project itself into the order of forms alone. And the fact that Klimt's art received the material support of a few wealthy patrons in no way changed its growing "lack of topicality" (cf. "My Kingdom is not of this World"). Thus the frieze signs the death warrant of the Secession, which the "Klimt group" (but this is mainly of anecdotal interest, like the opposition between the Naturalists, partisans of volume, and the Stylists, converted to flatness, which was the excuse for the break) left in 1905. On the brink of disaster, Klimt was saved only by the organization of the forms and signs in his pictures, whereas the Austrian "nation" was destined to experience the very real unleashing of the Hostile Powers.

A delicately balanced Faustian "lingering moment," an ambiguous high point of Art Nouveau, reaching for the hope of happiness, the Beethoven Frieze marks a tragic intermission. Held together by the internal balance and coherence resulting from the interaction of apparently contradictory elements, at the centre of the fascinating network of fables, figures and forms which meet in it, the frieze was momentarily "fixed" in the continuous unfolding of time and events by the will to art. For the annals of art history, Franz Wickhoff and Alois Riegl, in Vienna, then refused to foist on it the positivist "order" or the order of an aesthetic of the absolute. When all is said and done, the frieze, like all major works of art, inaugurates an order which is wholly its own.

Bibliography

Though parting company with them on some points of interpretation, the author is indebted to the essays of Alessandra Comini, Werner Hofmann and Carl E. Schorske; these are the best introduction to Klimt's work as a whole. He also owes a debt to the patient work of Marian Bisanz-Prakken, who has done much to elucidate the Beethoven Frieze.

XIV. Kunstausstellung der Vereinigung Bildender Künstler Österreichs Secession, Max Klinger, Beethoven, catalogue of the 14th Secession exhibition, Vienna, April-June 1902.

BAHR Hermann, *Gegen Klimt*, Vienna, 1903 (critical articles against Klimt, against the Beethoven Frieze in particular).

BISANZ-PRAKKEN Marian, "Zum Gemälde Pallas Athene von Klimt," in *Alte und moderne Kunst*, 21 (1976), No. 147, pp. 8-11.

— id. *Der Beethovenfries. Geschichte, Funktion und Bedeutung*, Salzburg 1977. New enlarged edition, Munich 1980.

— id. "Gustav Klimt und die 'Stilkunst' Jan Toorops," in *Klimt-Studien, Mitteilungen der Österreichischen Galerie*, 22-23 (1978-1979), No. 66-67, pp. 146-214.

— id. "Das Quadrat in der Flächenkunst der Wiener Secession," in *Alte und moderne Kunst*, 27 (1982), No. 180-181, pp. 40-46.

— id. "The Beethoven Exhibition of the Vienna Secession and the Younger Viennese Tradition of the Gesamtkunstwerk," in Erika NIELSEN (editor), *Focus on Vienna 1900*, Houston German Studies, No. 4, Munich 1982.

— id. "Programmatik und subjektive Aussage im Werk von Gustav Klimt," in Robert WAISSENBERGER (editor), *Wien 1870-1920, Traum und Wirklichkeit*, Salzburg 1984.

BOGNER Dieter, "Die geometrischen Reliefs von Josef Hoffmann," in *Alte und moderne Kunst*, 27 (1982), No. 184-185, pp. 24-32.

BOUILLON Jean-Paul, *Journal de l'Art Nouveau 1870-1914*, Geneva 1985. In English, *Art Nouveau 1870-1914*, New York and London 1985.

BREICHA Otto, *Gustav Klimt. Die goldene Pforte. Werk-Wesen-Wirkung*, Salzburg 1978, 2nd edition 1985 (critical anthology).

COMINI Alessandra, *Gustav Klimt*, New York 1975.

CORADESCHI Sergio, *L'opera completa di Klimt*, preface by Johannes Dobai, Milan 1978.

DOBAI Johannes, *Gustav Klimt*, preface by Fritz Novotny, Salzburg 1967, 2nd edition 1975. In English, London 1968 and Boston 1972 (complete catalogue of the paintings).

— id. "Zu Gustav Klimts Gemälde 'Der Kuss'," in *Mitteilungen der Österreichischen Galerie*, 12 (1968), No. 56.

HAMMER Ivo, "Il Fregio di Beethoven di Gustav Klimt," in *Le Arti a Vienna, dalla Secessione alla caduta dell'Impero asburgico*, exhibition catalogue, Venice Biennale, Palazzo Grassi, Venice 1984, pp. 107-113.

HEVESI Ludwig, *Acht Jahre Secession (März 1897-Juni 1905), Kritik-Polemik-Chronik*, Vienna 1906, reprinted 1985.

HOFMANN Werner, *Gustav Klimt und die Wiener Jahrhundertwende*, Salzburg 1970, reprinted 1977. In English, *Turning Points in Twentieth-Century Art: 1890-1917*, New York 1969.

— id. (editor), *Experiment Weltuntergang. Wien um 1900*, exhibition catalogue, Kunsthalle, Hamburg 1981.

KOLLER Manfred, "Klimts Beethovenfries – Zur Technologie und Erhaltung," in *Klimt-Studien. Mitteilungen der Österreichischen Galerie*, 22-23 (1978-1979), No. 66-67, pp. 215-240.

— id. "Monumentale Kunst um 1900 und heute. Der Beethovenfries von Gustav Klimt – Entstehung und Schicksal," in *Parnass*, 3 (1984).

LA GRANGE Henry-Louis de, *Gustav Mahler, chronique d'une vie*, Vol. II of *L'âge d'or de Vienne, 1900-1907*, Paris 1983.

NEBEHAY Christian M., *Gustav Klimt-Dokumentation*, Vienna 1969, new edition under the title *Gustav Klimt, Sein Leben nach zeitgenössischen Berichten und Quellen*, Munich 1976 (full documentation).

POLLAK Michael, *Vienne 1900, une identité blessée*, Paris 1984.

POWELL Nicolas, *The Sacred Spring. The Arts in Vienna 1898-1918*, London 1974.

SCHORSKE Carl E., *Fin-de-siècle Vienna, Politics and Culture*, London 1979 and New York 1980 (chapter 4 devoted to Klimt).

SEKLER Eduard F., "Mackintosh und Wien," in *Charles R. Mackintosh*, exhibition catalogue, Vienna 1969. In English in J.M. RICHARDS and Nikolaus PEVSNER (editors), *The Anti-Rationalists. Art Nouveau Architecture and Design*, Toronto and London 1973.

— id. *Josef Hoffmann, Das architektonische Werk*, Salzburg and Vienna 1982. In English, *Josef Hoffmann: The Architectural Work*, Princeton and London 1985.

STROBL Alice, "Zu den Fakultätsbildern von Gustav Klimt," in *Albertina Studien II*, 1964, pp. 138-169.

— id. *Gustav Klimt, Die Zeichnungen I (1878-1903)*, Salzburg 1980 (catalogue of the drawings).

Traum und Wirklichkeit – Wien 1870-1930, exhibition catalogue, Historisches Museum der Stadt Wien, Vienna 1985 (chapter 16 devoted to the Beethoven Frieze, with essays by M. Bisanz-Prakken, I. Hammer, M. Koller and H. Hollein).

VERGO Peter, "Gustav Klimt's Beethoven Frieze," in *The Burlington Magazine*, CXV (February 1973), No. 839, pp. 109-113.

— id. *Art in Vienna 1898-1918. Klimt, Kokoschka, Schiele and Their Contemporaries*, London 1975, 2nd edition 1981.

WAISSENBERGER Robert, *Die Wiener Secession*, Vienna 1971.

— id. (editor), *Wien 1890-1920*, Fribourg (Switzerland) 1984. In English, *Vienna 1890-1920*, New York and London 1984.

List of illustrations

Oil paintings

PHOTOGRAPHS AND DOCUMENTS

Contents

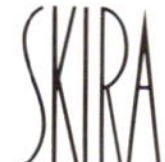

Printed by
IRL Imprimeries Réunies Lausanne s.a.

Published in the United States of America in 1987 by
RIZZOLI INTERNATIONAL PUBLICATIONS, INC.
597 Fifth Avenue/New York 10017

Translated from the French by Michael Heron

Library of Congress Cataloging-in-Publication Data

Bouillon, Jean Paul.
Klimt: Beethoven: the frieze for the Ninth symphony.

Bibliography: p.
1. Klimt, Gustav, 1862-1918. Beethoven frieze.
2. Wiener Secession. 3. Beethoven, Ludwig van, 1770-1827—Influence. I. Title.
ND511.5.K55A6213 1987 759.36 86-43220
ISBN 0-8478-0814-9 (pbk.)

Author and publisher take pleasure in recording their grateful thanks to Madame Erich Lederer, Geneva, Herr Dr. Gerbert Frodl of the Österreichische Galerie, Vienna, and Herr Franz Eder of Galerie Welz, Salzburg, who have kindly given permission to reproduce the works in their collections, and whose ready cooperation in many details of research has been most helpful in the making of this book.

Printed in Switzerland